I0074620

TAKE IT OFF.

A STORY OF ONE MAN *SPENDING* HIS WAY THROUGH LIFE… UNTIL HE **CHOSE** TO **INVEST** IN THE **REST** OF IT

By

Matthew David Grishman

7 SQUARED, LLC

7 SQUARED, LLC
3470 MOUNT DIABLO BOULEVARD
SUITE A210
LAFAYETTE, CA 94549

COPYRIGHT © 2015 BY MATTHEW GRISHMAN
COVER DESIGN BY PIA BERTONE-GROSS
ILLUSTRATIONS BY PIA BERTONE-GROSS

ALL RIGHTS RESERVED

FOR INFORMATION ABOUT SPECIAL DISCOUNTS FOR BULK
PURCHASES, PLEASE EMAIL INFO@TAKEITOFFTHEBOOK.COM

ISBN: 978-0-9971571-1-6

WRITTEN BY MATTHEW D. GRISHMAN
FORWARD WRITTEN BY JAMES C. GEBHARDT, CFP®

PRINTED IN THE UNITED STATES OF AMERICA

This book is dedicated to those professionals who work like cobblers on everyone's shoes but their own. I'm here for you. I'm here to listen to your story if you need someone to tell it to. If you're still wearing a mask, I'm here to help you take it off and live the authentic life you deserve.

~ Matthew D. Grishman, Author

FORWARD

HAVE YOU SEEN MY BLIND SPOT?

By Jim Gebhardt, CFP®

Will it ever rain again in California? Will the Chicago Cubs ever win another World Series? Will the stock market ever go down again?

At the time I was asked by my dear friend and colleague, Matthew Grishman, to write the forward for <u>TAKE IT OFF</u>, the current trends all said "no" to these questions. However, is "no" the real answer, or is it an illusion created entirely by the *human blind spot*?

Shortly after graduating college, I found myself sitting by the window of my basement apartment in Rochester, NY, unable to see the street because several feet of snow had buried me in my home for days. It felt like winter would never end. Therefore I packed up my stuff, drove the treacherous road to my office, and demanded my boss authorize a work transfer to California.

When I finally reached the land of eternal sunshine, it was 1993 and California had just begun recovering from the economic recession of 1991. Real estate values had plummeted, Bill Clinton was just inaugurated into the White House, violent extremists bombed the World Trade Center in New York City, a devastating tsunami caused by an Earthquake off Hokkaido, Japan killed 202 people, the ever popular Beanie Babies hit store shelves, the first bagless vacuum cleaner was invented, Intel introduced the Pentium Processor, and Whitney Houston's "I

Will Always Love You" reached number one on the music charts; all of this seems like a lifetime ago!

My first job in California was working as a surety bond underwriter for one of the largest insurance companies in the country. It was my daily duty to dive into the balance sheets and financial statements of the various construction companies our firm bonded. It was a mundane job for an aspiring 23-year-old, but the knowledge I gained from studying these balance sheets was invaluable for the work I do today.

One common holding I came across on our clients' corporate balance sheets was investments in real estate. With real estate values still significantly depressed following the 1991 recession, our clients were often struggling to keep their investment properties in good financial standing. As a young analyst I often wondered, *"Why didn't these business owners prepare for an economic downturn by building up some emergency cash?"*

As I interviewed these business owners, I learned quickly that as their investments became more and more valuable, they could never envision a downturn in real estate values; ever! To my surprise, the opposite now held true; these business owners could not see a time when their depressed real estate holdings would ever recover; ever! Most of my clients were ready to liquidate their real estate, assume a large loss on their investment, and move on while they licked their wounds. It was as if they had completely forgotten what it was like to see their real estate values appreciate.

This observation, as a bond underwriter in my early twenties, helped me really understand how the majority of people make investment decisions. For the past twenty years as a financial advisor, I have witnessed firsthand how very difficult it is for most human beings to envision a future reversal in the direction of current trends occurring in their lives.

The lack of significant rain in California these past few years has made it difficult to imagine anything but drought going forward. Real estate values, which were decimated in the 2008 recession, have been on a tear the past few years. It seems as though they will never languish again! The stock market has also been on a virtual straight line upward since 2009, causing most people I meet to forget what it feels like to lose money, thus being highly unprepared for the next bear market. Conversely, after spending many late nights with clients throughout 2008, most could not envision a time when the global financial crisis would ever end. My clients truly believed they would never be able to have the happy retirement we had just spent a decade or more helping them plan for.

This phenomenon, which I have seen over and over, is what I refer to as one of our biggest every day blind spots; assuming the current trend in life will go on indefinitely, therefore leaving us completely unprepared for the inevitable trend change that will occur at some point in the future. This is the main reason why most investors make terrible mistakes with their money. Emotion (mainly fear or greed) takes over the decision-making process because of the irrational belief that the current trend will never end. Investors often see an exciting upward trend in the market and dump all of their money into very speculative investments, assuming the trend or fad will continue upward forever. This was vividly seen when warnings of a tech bubble implosion was completely ignored by investors in the late 1990's. New money poured into technology stocks and technology mutual funds in the fourth quarter of 1999 and the first quarter of 2000, after nearly a decade-long run-up in prices. Despite the implosion of the bubble that began in March of 2000, few investors believed a real trend reversal had just occurred. Most believed technology stocks and funds would continue to go higher and higher despite the March pullback. Those who could not envision and plan for a different direction other than upward, were soon awoken to a harsh reality; that market trends do change, and when they do, they can wipe out everything you have.

As an experienced student of trend analysis, my team and I have built a comprehensive instrument panel to assist us in identifying potential trend reversals in every sector of the global market. Our team then makes investment decisions based on the output of this instrument panel.

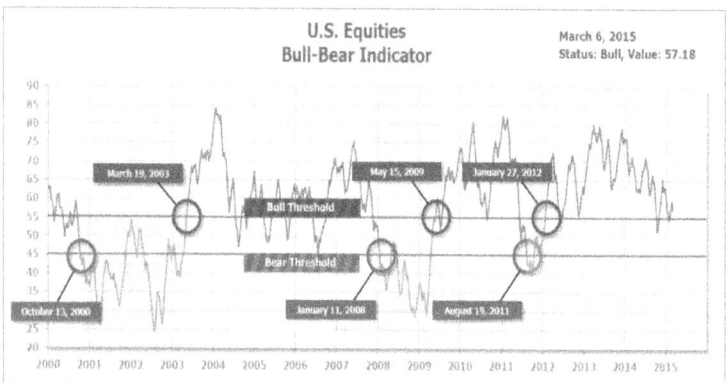

This chart represents one of our three primary indicators as of March 6, 2015. You will notice when our instrument panel indicated trend reversals in US markets going back to the internet bubble of 2000. You should specifically pay attention to the trend reversals our indicators identified on January 11, 2008 and May 15, 2009. On January 11, 2008, our indicators signaled a trend reversal after a huge run up in stock prices. Without any emotion or second guessing, our indicators told us to enter *protect mode* and move the majority of our clients' assets to cash. Then again on May 15, 2009, after experiencing the worst recession since the 1920's, our indicators signaled another reversal to *growth mode,* instructing a full re-entry to the markets. During both trend reversals, most investors were stuck in their *blind spot*, unable to see a direction other than the current uptrend or downtrend we had been experiencing. The effect for most was a devastating loss or a missed opportunity.

Every human being has blind spots; it's part of our nature. For most of us, our first awareness of blind spots comes from the first time we get behind the wheel of a car with our driving instructor sitting beside us.

"Don't forget to check your blind spots," the instructor tells us.

In fact, our driving instructor may be one of the few teachers to help us become acutely aware and actively in search of blind spots. Unfortunately, we do not often identify the other blind spots in life and we allow them to jump out and surprise us, often with significant and unpleasant consequences.

Imagine the different outcome that could have occurred for the construction company owners I worked with 22 years ago. What might have happened had they been aware of their blind spots with their real estate investments? Had they seen the possibility of trend reversals and prepared for them, they would have been able to keep their real estate holdings while profiting incredibly when values rebounded. Instead, their blind spots led many of them to financial ruin by selling at historically low prices.

Since, by definition, a blind spot is something we are not capable of seeing on our own, we must hire trained professionals to help us identify, address and eliminate them. People I meet do this in many areas of their lives:

- The home inspector who makes you aware of a termite infestation that could devastate your home's foundation.

- The mechanic who tells you your rear brakes need replacing before you get in a terrible accident.

- The accountant who identifies the opportunity for a large tax refund rather than the IRS keeping more of your money than necessary.

Do you have someone helping you identify your blind spots with your finances? Do you have someone helping you see your blind spots in how you measure your true wealth?

In the following pages, Matthew will take you on a journey of identifying blind spots that go deep into how our society has generally misunderstood the meaning of true wealth. Matthew's personal stories will make you aware of your blind spots and how to take the steps necessary to create and preserve a truly wealthy, happy life.

- Will it ever rain again in California?

- Will the Chicago Cubs ever win another World Series?

- Will the stock market ever go down again?

- Will you ever find true happiness and abundance in this world of scarcity?

The real question is will you ignore these possibilities by allowing them to remain in your blind spot? Or will you read on and become more aware of the ways you're not "seeing" possible outcomes that could drastically change your life?

The choice is yours to make.

PART I:

THE MASK

ROCKSTARS REQUIREment

1 TAILORED PINSTRIPE SUIT
2 CRISP WHITE BUTTON-DOWN
3 WING TIPS
4 SUPERLATIVE BLING
5 MONOGRAMMED CUFFLINKS
6 SEXY EUROPEAN CARS

A colleague made a comment on one of my LinkedIn posts that really caught my attention. My friend is an old pro in the financial services industry and someone I've known for more than fifteen years.

He typed, "Matt, we work like cobblers on everyone else's shoes except our own."

This was certainly not the first time I had heard this, but for some reason, this time the reminder stopped me and I began to think about my own career.

For most of my twenty years as a financial professional, my personal finances were a mess. I'd been aware of this for a long time, but for some reason, hearing my friend's reminder that day gave me the spark to sit down and write this book. It scared the heck out of me to know that I was going to be telling some very personal stories to a potentially large audience. But I wanted to do it anyway. If my experiences can help even one person avoid the expensive and painful mistakes I have made, it will be worth it.

And so, here is the story of how I went from spending my way through life to choosing to invest in the rest of it.

It was 1995 and all I wanted to be was rich...filthy rich. The potential fame and fortune of working as a stock broker on Wall Street drew me in at the age of twenty-one.

I remember my first branch manager, Jeff Nielson, telling me, "Listen here, Rookie. You wanna make it in this business?"

"Of course, Mr. Nielson," I responded.

"Then get your ass married as soon as possible, pump out a few kids, buy a big house you can't afford, and get a hot set of wheels you can't afford either. That's my guarantee you'll show up to work every day and dial for dollars."

As the first new trainee in my firm's Darien, Connecticut office in several years, I was surrounded by fast-talking, stock-pitching, IPO-slinging hot shots. Everyone drove a Benz or a BMW and kept a collection of monogrammed French cuff shirts hanging in the closet of their office. My manager's advice seemed dead on. But since I wasn't convinced I was cut out for being a broker, I took my time with Jeff's "shopping list" for starving young pros.

Sure enough, after dialing my phone over 300 times a day for an entire year, I was ready to call it quits. I absolutely detested cold calling. And no matter how much allure the lifestyle around me had, I couldn't motivate myself to pick up the phone and hear one more person say *"Hell no! Go away and don't call me again!"*

With results like that, how was I going to find my fame and fortune and finally realize my dream of living like a rock star? I was days away from resigning as a broker and I had no idea what would be next for me.

And then *next* showed up.

Paul Smith walked into my office one Tuesday morning, and by the time he left that afternoon he had made me an offer I could hardly resist. Paul was a young sales rep for an up- and-coming mutual fund firm based in New York City. He was twenty-seven years old and delivered a presentation to the brokers in my office that had me hanging on every word. Since I knew little about mutual funds, I really didn't understand what he was talking about. But man, did he sound smooth. And he looked like a million bucks. He wore a sharp pinstripe suit with a crisp white button down and the shiniest wing tip shoes I had ever seen. He didn't look like the guys in my office, with their French cuffs and absurdly loud ties. Rather, he looked like a real pro from Wall Street: not overdressed, but simply understated and striking.

After the presentation, I asked Paul to visit with me in my office.

"Paul, tell me how you got into wholesaling for a mutual fund company?" I asked.

"Simple," he said. "I saw an ad in the *New York Times* about internal sales jobs at [the firm]. I interviewed. I got hired. Two years later, I was relocated to Boston and got my own territory to run."

Paul spent an hour and a half answering all of my questions about his life as a mutual fund wholesaler. It sounded too good to be true. Paul lived in the Back Bay of Boston in a very nice condo. He made just over $250,000 a year traveling around the Northeast meeting with brokers like me every day. His firm gave him amazing benefits and a six-figure travel and entertainment budget.

The more Paul spoke, the more I knew this was the job for me. I was done living on my $400 a week draw and eating ramen noodles for dinner every night. It was time.

"Guess what, Matt?" Paul said, as if reading my mind. "We're hiring."

Paul told me that his company needed trainees to work in their Manhattan office, and one day, move out into their own territory somewhere in the U.S., doing exactly what Paul was doing.

"Are you serious?" I was incredulous.

I begged him for an introduction to his company, and Paul obliged. That afternoon I bought myself a navy pinstripe suit, polished my resume (and my wingtips), and prepared for that moment when I would head off to New York to explore my new career options as a wholesaler in the financial services industry.

Fast forward seventeen years, and life as a wholesaler was everything I had imagined it would be. I became a senior vice president and a national spokesperson for one of the largest insurance companies in the world.

For nearly all the years I wholesaled mutual funds and insurance products, I made the big bucks. I wore $2,000 suits and owned a fancy collection of Rolex watches. I drove sexy European cars and only traveled first class. I was pampered with outstanding meals and drank $300 bottles of wine every day like they were cans of Budweiser. I got married to the most beautiful woman in the world, built her a giant house, and had a couple of kids (just like Jon advised me). From birth my kids wore designer clothing and my wife, Amie, was able to spend without the burden of a monthly budget.

I had arrived.

I found my way to the top by learning how to tell a great story, by inspiring enthusiasm in everyone I met, and by strutting down the street like I was the man. I had everything I had ever wanted: money, power, respect, and a smoking-hot wife. I was finally living the life of an absolute rock star--the real American dream--at the top of the financial food chain.

Or so I thought.

One morning in the summer of 2005, as I was standing in my bathroom, admiring myself in the mirror, the walls around me came tumbling down. My life as a big shot was about to come to an abrupt end. I was waiting for a limo to pick me up. I was two hours away from boarding a flight to southern California, where I was scheduled to speak for my firm at a large industry conference at the San Diego Convention Center.

Just then, my wife Amie reminded me to stop at the bank on my way to the airport to get out some cash, since I had forgotten to do so the day before.

I quickly scanned my bank account balance on my laptop to see which account I needed to get the money from.

Holy crap! I thought.

My accounts were overdrawn by over two hundred dollars. That had to be a bank mistake. There was no way that could happen. Amie would have to handle that as I was on my way out of town.

The solution was simple: a cash advance from one of my five credit cards. But as I checked one card after another, I saw that all five had been maxed out.

I was stunned.

I knew I had been charging up a storm and throwing cash around like it grew on a tree in my back yard, but up until now, I had been unaware of the spending damage I had done. To top it all off, I was not getting paid for another three weeks.

I realized that morning that I had zero purchasing power. Yet I was supposed to fly to San Diego and represent one of the largest insurance and annuity companies on Earth in front of a room full of financial advisors.

My heart started pounding in my chest. Sweat began pouring down my face onto my handmade silk tie. My vision blurred and all I could see was a dark tunnel. Was that light at the end of it, or the train headed my way?

My knees eventually gave out and I fell to the floor. Was I having a heart attack?

I lay on the floor in my Hickey Freeman suit, feeling like I was going to die. As the panic completely overwhelmed me, I called Amie into the bathroom and told her what was happening.

"Honey, how the hell am I going to check into my hotel tonight? How am I going to pay for a cab from the airport to my hotel? How am I going to eat?"

Amie didn't have an answer. She just began to cry. And I began to panic.

I pulled my phone out of pocket and called my boss.

"John, I can't make it to San Diego."

"What?" he shouted.

In my best false sick voice, I muttered, "I'm sick as a dog. I woke up with a stomach bug and I can't board a plane, let alone leave my bathroom. I think I have the flu."

"Oh man, that's horrible," John said. "Okay. Feel better and take care of yourself. We'll find a speaker. Not as good as you, of course, but we'll figure out Plan B."

At the time, I felt I had no choice but to tell my boss this whopping story. And he bought it. Temporary relief was mine. But as I hung up the phone, it dawned on me that my entire life as a corporate big shot was one big lie.

My anxiety began to escalate as the combined reality of being broke and completely full of shit most of my life started to sink in. I had led everyone to believe I had the world at my feet. Yet there I was; a useless puddle of failure, curled up on my bathroom floor in my $2,000 suit.

I did not have the financial means to gas up my car, or buy groceries, or even make the co-pay at the pediatrician if my kids got sick. I already owed my parents close to fifty grand for bailing me out of a housing mess in 2002, so there was no way I was going to call them for more help. I was way too embarrassed to call any of my colleagues or friends.

For God's sake, here I had been making a high six-figure income for more than a decade, helping financial advisors make better investment decisions for their clients, and I was flat-out broke.

Maybe I was just flat-out broken.

I had to think. I had to figure something out.

All I could do was jump in my car and go for a drive.

As I rode recklessly around town, I couldn't come up with any logical answers. I was blowing through red lights and stop signs, speeding, cutting off other drivers, oblivious to the world around me. It was a miracle I didn't kill anyone. My brain was spinning in circles and I kept looking at myself in the rear-view mirror.

"You are such a jerk. You are a complete idiot!" I said to myself.

I felt like the worst human being on the planet. I began wondering if I should just veer into oncoming traffic or drive off a high embankment. At least then my wife and kids would collect my $4 million in life insurance and everything would be okay for them financially. The hurt and disgust would go away for me, too. But every time I tried to steer my car into oncoming traffic, I couldn't do it.

Jesus Christ! I couldn't even kill myself if I wanted to.

Nothing in my life was within my control. Everything was insane and I had no answers. I felt completely hopeless.

With my gas tank running low, I gave up my quest for solutions and headed home to beg for my wife's forgiveness. I walked in the front door and it was obvious that she was scared and angry. Amie, the most beautiful creature in existence, with tears puddling under her eyes, sat clutching our two boys while they cried in her arms. Miles, who was five at the time, was holding his favorite stuffed puppy, and Lucas, my little munchkin, was wedged between them in his Toy Story pajamas.

"Where were you, Daddy?" Miles asked.

Before I could mutter an answer, Amie shouted, "I can't believe it. We're out of money? Are you kidding me?"

"I'm so sorry, honey. I'm so sorry. I'll fix this. I promise."

The yelling and crying continued on for hours, until exhaustion took over and a temporary truce was declared. It was our decision to hunker down at home for a few weeks with just our family of four.

We were going to figure out how we got into this mess and how we were going to get out of it.

So there we sat, for three whole weeks.

We didn't go out. We didn't see friends. Amie and I finally came to some agreement about what we needed to do. We decided we were going to be very open with our kids, involving them in much of our discussion. Despite the kids still being very young, it was important to me that they know that I messed up, that I had made millions of dollars and squandered most of it on meaningless stuff. It was important for them also to know that I was going to own my mistakes and do whatever it took to fix them.

It was during that time that I first began to understand the true meaning of wealth.

One day Miles, who, as I've said, was only five, looked at me and said, "Dad, we're a family and that's more important than money. I'll always love you no matter what. Do you need a hug?"

The tears could not be held back. I cried harder than I ever had in my life.

I called one of my closest friends, who happened to be a financial advisor, and I begged him for his help. He was only one I could trust.

"What's up? What do you need?" Jim asked.

Thankfully, Jim was willing and able to help us, and we were willing to do whatever he told us to do.

Jim started us on an "austerity diet." I was never good at dieting, but I was out of options. No more frivolous spending. No more expensive dinners.

But as I was to learn, my spending was really just a symptom of a much larger demon brewing inside me. Jim introduced me to his life coach, Jim Kelly. It was on our very first call together that I heard the question that would change the entire direction of my life.

Jim Kelly asked me point blank, "Matthew, when are you going to stop lying and start telling the truth to yourself and the whole world?"

I said, "To hell with you!" and hung up the phone.

The truth hurt.

Yet despite my denial, I felt something inside me begin to shift. Within a few minutes of slamming the phone down on Jim, I called him back.

"I'm so sorry, Jim. I didn't mean to hang up on you like a complete jerk. Please tell me more about what you just said to me."

Jim responded gently, with a slight chuckle in his voice. "Take it off, Matthew."

"Take what off?" I asked.

Jim said, "The mask you've been wearing your whole life. Take it off and let the world see the beautiful, imperfect *you* that it's been waiting for."

As scary as that was even to consider, I realized at that moment that most of my life had been in fact spent hiding. The way I dressed, the way I acted, the way I carried myself every day…it was all one big facade that obscured the real me.

I wasn't exactly sure why I made the choice to hide behind my mask, but I knew it was time to take it off.

By 2007, two years after hitting rock bottom, I felt as if I had the foundation in place to turn my life around. I didn't hate myself like I used to. I was telling the truth to myself and others. I had reached an all-new high point in my self-esteem after earning the most money I had ever earned in my career. It wasn't the big paycheck that made me stand taller; it was what I did with the paycheck that made me feel really good about myself.

New money habits were firmly taking root in me. When it was time to replace my seven-year-old Audi, rather than leasing another new German car as I would have in my rock star days, I purchased a used Ford Crown Victoria for $11,400. And I paid cash. I got teased by my of old colleagues and clients, but that choice to drive within my means was well worth the temporary torment I received from others.

I even remember one client saying to me, "Dude, are they not paying you anymore?"

I responded, "Yes, of course they're paying me. In fact more money than I've ever earned. It's just that I put my money in the bank rather than seeing it depreciate in a ridiculous car."

I learned throughout this entire ordeal that there are two kinds of pain in this world: the pain of discipline and the pain of regret. And I learned you can only avoid one kind, so going forward I would choose more carefully. I had lived with the excruciating pain of regret for so many years.

Choosing the pain of discipline and allowing our advisor, Jim, to hold us accountable, Amie and I were able to completely reverse course and build the kind of true wealth we had always dreamed about. So much so that in 2011, I was able to walk away from corporate America and do what it was I was really meant to do:

BECOME THE BEST WEALTH COACH IN THE BUSINESS, HELPING OTHER PEOPLE LIKE ME LEARN HOW TO FORGIVE THEMSELVES, LOVE THEMSELVES, CHANGE HABITS, AND MOVE FORWARD IN LIFE WITH THE CLARITY AND THE GAME-PLAN FOR HOW TO BUILD AND PROTECT THEIR TRUE WEALTH.

By telling my stories and becoming completely vulnerable to the world, I healed from the wounds of my past and have since helped others take that first step in doing the same. When talking with others about their experiences, a question continues to come up in almost every conversation.

"Matt, what the heck happened in your life that led you down this path? Why did you feel the need to lie to the whole world and make up this rock star image of who you thought the world wanted to know? When did you put your mask on?"

This is what I tell them.

At ten years old, I was the target of two bullies on the playground of my elementary school. Their names were Gerry and Joe.

I was different from these boys. I was a Jewish kid from New York City with affluent, well-educated parents. Here we were, living in a small farming community in upstate New York that had never seen a real live Jewish kid before (or so it seemed). My Dad was the superintendent of schools and one of the highest-paid people in town. As a public figure, his salary was published annually in the local newspaper.

Day after day, these two bullies tormented me. Some days they threw anti-Semitic slurs in my face; other days it was their fists. Every day in fifth and sixth grade, I was chased around the playground while all the other kids just watched and laughed.

"Where you running to, Jew Boy?" they used to say. "Hey! Come here, Jew. I want to see if you have horns on your forehead like all Jews."

I was confused, and I was afraid. I thought that if I told my teacher, they would surely kill me.

I tried to talk to my dad, but he was so busy with his job that all he could say was, "If someone is attacking you, hit them back. If that doesn't work, tell your teacher."

I had no choice. I was going to have to face these guys one day and put an end to the bullying.

That day finally came a couple years later while my dad and I were standing on the fifty-yard line of our high school football game. Gerry and Joe walked up to me where I was watching with my dad.

Gerry had this stupid grin on his face. "Hey Jew boy," he said. "Wanna fight?"

"No," I responded.

"Well, we're going to kick your ass tonight anyway. So either fight back or lay there like a weak little Jew and take your beating."

I had had enough. I looked over at my Dad, who had no idea this was going on, shook my head, and followed Gerry and Joe to the parking lot of the high school. Something in me had snapped.

"You ready, Jew? You're dead meat," said Gerry.

As he lunged toward me, I cocked my arm back and hit him as hard as I could in the stomach. A loud, long breath came spewing out of his mouth as he dropped like a pile of bricks onto the pavement.

Joe looked at me with a horrific stare. My heart was throbbing in my throat and I got very dizzy. I couldn't believe what I had just done.

As I stood there stunned with my mouth gapped open, Joe picked Gerry up off the ground, slung him over his shoulder and ran. I could hear Joe's clomping feet and Gerry's gasps for air gradually fade as they disappeared into the woods behind the high school.

That was finally the end of three hostile years of bullying by Gerry and Joe. *And I made a decision that I would never let this happen to me again.*

Rather than being myself and taking the risk that someone else might bully me for it, I decided to hide from the world. By age twelve I had made a conscious choice not to let the world see me for who I really was. I was going to create a mask, a persona that blended me in with everyone else. In fact, behind my mask, I was going to exemplify "normalcy" by being the coolest, smartest, bravest kid in my school, even if that meant making up stories and telling flat-out lies.

At the end of ninth grade, my dad got a new job far from the hell hole we lived in during my days of being bullied. There I met new kids and began making friends immediately. My mask-wearing strategy was working. On the outside, everyone at my new school began to adore me. They saw this fifteen-year-old Renaissance "man" who came from wealth and already traveled the world (mostly through fictional stories I created in my head). I quickly became the center of the party, and all the cool kids wanted to hang out with me.

As I grew older, finished college and began making some serious money, my life as a rock star reached a new level. Every weekend was spent partying like it was New Year's Eve, and I paid the bill. To keep my mask on and keep the party going, I had to throw money around and continue creating stories that wowed my growing circle of followers.

Despite all the comfort I had bought myself and all the fun I was having, I felt completely empty inside. My spending grew to epic proportions, fueled in large part by alcohol and drugs, which became my regular pain killers for the hurt I was feeling inside. The life of the mask-yielding rock star hit all new false heights. The entire world saw the epitome of success; all I saw was a lying, worthless failure.

Until that disastrous day in 2005, I showed the world who I wanted them to see. And it was from the financial tragedy that almost destroyed my family that I took my first step forward. I started by telling the truth and letting the world see the real me: a far-from-perfect, bullied kid who still makes mistakes every day, and feels sadness and anger as often as he feels happiness and excitement. Identifying that trigger moment in my life and choosing to move forward with courage, forgiveness, and gratitude (and a lot of help from the people whom I love) is what brought me to tell my most personal stories.

Here I sit in 2016, just eleven years after considering suicide, feeling proud and accomplished with what I've built. I am a very wealthy man who lives in a modest house, drives a base model pick-up truck, and arrives at work most days wearing shorts and sneakers. I have completely redefined what true wealth means to me. It's not just about money anymore. It's about the four most important components of my life: my family, my occupation, my recreation, and my beliefs about money.

- My *family* is rock solid and I am surrounded by the people I love.

- My *occupation* gives me purpose as I make a difference in the lives of those I serve.

- ***Recreation*** is an everyday occurrence. I have fun doing the things I love with the people I love in my favorite places.

And I have developed a belief system about ***money.*** Money is a precious resource; I have learned how to save it and use it for the really important things in life, like vacationing with my family, educating my kids, and building a business that employs and helps others in my community.

Am I perfect? Not even close. Even as the owner of a wealth management firm, I still make stupid mistakes with my money. Last spring I bought an Apple watch because it looked really cool. Now it sits on my nightstand collecting dust. What a waste of four hundred dollars!

I still fall off the wagon every once in a while, but I guess that's part of being human. Thankfully, Amie believes in me and accepts me fully for who I am. My boys fill my heart with endless amounts of gratitude as they remind me every day of the simple gifts of love and laughter. My Mom, Jill, my Dad, Hank, and my brother, Daniel, have always shown me unconditional love and encouragement, despite my many lies to them over nearly three decades. And finally, I still have my dearest friend and financial advisor, Jim Gebhardt, in my life. Jim happens to be my business partner now, working by my side inspiring me every day so I can do the work I was meant to do for others.

I will forever be grateful for Jim Kelly, the incredibly kind and patient coach who showed me the meaning of authenticity. Despite passing away a few years ago, his light shines genuinely through me every day.

I chose to write this book and tell some very personal stories in a public forum for my former colleagues, friends, and the millions of other hard working people who are quietly suffering as I did. I hope you'll join me on a journey of discovery that's all about the meaning of true wealth, and how you can learn from my experience to get there.

Here's what you'll find in the remaining chapters of this book.

- Part II, *Short Stories about Life, Leadership, Parenting and True Wealth,* begins our journey with personal and family stories that helped me understand and define the meaning of true wealth.

- Part III, *Building and Protecting Wealth*, is loaded with sound bites and anecdotes for building wealth from the ground up, one step at a time.

- Part IV, *A New Approach to Protecting and Growing Money*, introduces some 21st-century thinking about creating and preserving wealth. You will be invited to enter a whole new dimension for achieving true wealth and happiness.

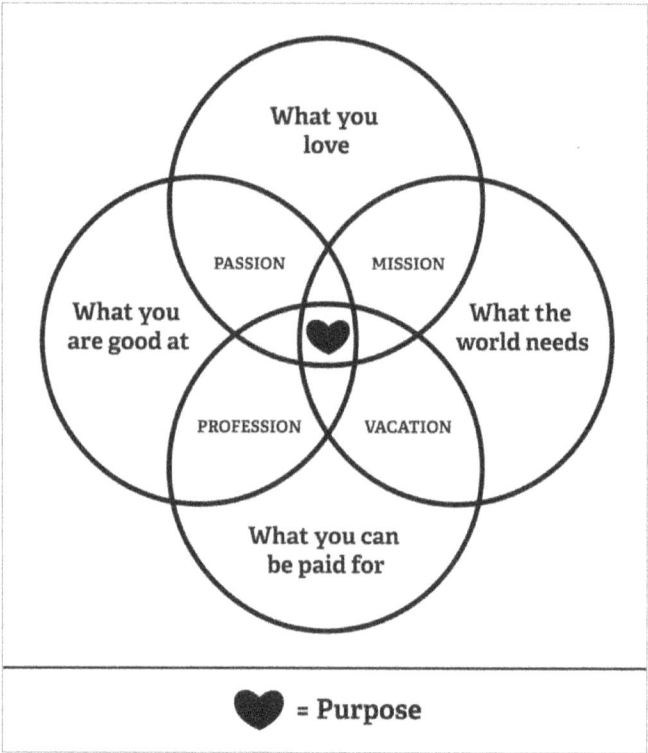

What you
love

PASSION   MISSION

What you   ♥   What the
are good at   world needs

PROFESSION   VACATION

What you can
be paid for

♥ = Purpose

PART II

SHORT STORIES ABOUT LIFE, LEADERSHIP, PARENTING AND TRUE WEALTH

We continue our journey together by sharing lessons learned through the school of hard knocks. In this section of the book, I'll discuss philosophical beliefs I've developed about living a wealthy life, based on real life experiences and challenges that were fought along the way.

Everyone needs to learn the hard way sometimes, but if I can help one person avoid a terrible financial mistake because I shared a personal experience, then writing this part of the book was well worth it.

On November 17, 2011, my father-in-law, Alan "Pa" Lanzendorf, lost a long battle with pulmonary fibrosis. It was an incredibly sad time in my life. I had lost one of the greatest teachers I had ever known. Since then, I have spent a great amount of time reflecting on our twenty-one years together and all the things I learned from his amazing life and remarkable stories.

Pa was a brilliant man. He started his collegiate years at sixteen years old at Tufts University. But since his dad only agreed to pay for two years of college and it was now his brothers' turn to go, Pa was forced to drop out and join the Army.

After an honorable discharge and thanks to the GI Bill, Pa was able to return to college and earn his degree from Syracuse University in 1957. He dreamed of being a park ranger in one of our national parks like Yosemite or Yellowstone. In fact, Pa really could have been anything he wanted to be, whether a military officer, doctor, lawyer, or rocket scientist.

But life took over and Pa fell in love with being a husband and father. He chose a nine-to-five job working for the state of New York, first in the conservation department, then as an analyst for the Department of Criminal Justice. That job choice turned into a 35-year career that allowed him to be home every night for dinner. He never traveled for work. He never interrupted his family time to take a call from his boss.

Money was never his passion, yet Pa always seemed to have enough. His wife, Carol, was dedicated to staying home to care for the four kids. Together they created a warm, safe home with food on the table, clothes on everyone's backs, and top-notch college educations for their kids. All four now have loving, prosperous lives with families of their own.

Pa was a man of devout faith, and it was really the simple things that he enjoyed most. Pa believed in God, put on his best suit, and attended church every Sunday. He told me countless stories of Boy Scout camping with his boys and the Sunday drives the family would take after church. But as he got older, his greatest joy came from walks with Carol, reading his newspaper, playing on the floor with his grandkids, and having long talks with just about anyone.

I was one of the lucky ones that got to spend hours and hours in conversation with Pa, listening to the stories of his life and all the amazing people he met, as well as all of the personal difficulties he had to overcome growing up. Yet despite the challenges that would have made most people resentful in life, Pa always treated others with incredible kindness and compassion. Whether with family or a complete stranger, Pa was genuinely interested in people, and they knew it from the minute he said hello. He expressed empathy unlike anyone else I had ever known. He was a truly gentle, loving soul.

Pa is the wealthiest man I have ever known. He was never rich in money or possessions. He was grounded in his love for his family, the simplicity of his fun, and the work ethic he possessed and carried for nearly forty years.

It is this wealth he has passed on to me--the most valuable inheritance I could have ever received.

In my role as a wealth advisor, I meet many "wealthy" people who are completely broke when it comes to true wealth. Many tortured souls arrive in my office with more money than most people could spend in eight lifetimes, yet they are unhappy at work, they are at odds with their spouses, their kids are often a mess, and they feel completely stuck. What I inherited from Pa has helped me connect deeply with people like this.

I am incredibly grateful every day for the work I do in my business; helping people define, develop and protect their true wealth...not just their financial riches.

THE COMPONENTS OF TRUE WEALTH

Family

The largest component of true wealth is *family*.

Who are the most important people in your life? Identify them. Cherish them. Offer them love, compassion and forgiveness.

Occupation

How do you give your gifts to your community and the world? Do you work? Volunteer? Coach?

In our office, we believe in giving before getting. Identifying what inspires you to contribute to your community is a critical part of measuring one's true wealth.

Recreation

How do you like to have fun? Most people we meet find that it is often the simplest things in life that generate the most fun, especially if these activities involve family and the people you care most about. Family trips, taking a walk, family movie night, dinner out with friends, or going to a ball game are all things clients tell us are their favorite fun things to do, and none of them require a lot of money. Yet they enhance one's true wealth at a core happiness level.

Money

How does money serve you? What is your belief system surrounding money?

We meet many people with sizable assets who often lack clarity on how their money serves their most important aspirations. They often tell us they earn plenty of income but don't know where it all goes at the end of the month. We also come across people who spend a lot of time and energy preparing a financial estate for their heirs, yet they do not spend an equal amount of time preparing their heirs for the estate; and it is often squandered quickly on meaningless "stuff."

Having a written belief system for you and your family to follow when it comes to the meaning of your true wealth protects your money—and, more importantly, your belief system-- for generations.

Have you measured your true wealth?

True wealth means so much more than having a large financial estate. True wealth is measured by your relationship with family, occupation, recreation, and money. Having a healthy understanding of this can allow for greater fulfillment and happiness in life.

I have dedicated myself and my occupation to helping families identify, manage, protect, and pass on their true wealth.

This is the greatest gift I received from Pa, and I am forever grateful to be able to share this gift with others in need.

Pa would want it no other way.

My dad is my hero.

I am so full of pride to be the son of Henry Grishman. From the time I was a young boy, I wanted to spend every minute I could with him. I wanted to dress like he dressed. I wanted to talk like he talked. I wanted to inspire people the way he did. I wanted to be able to fix things like he fixed them. I wanted to *be* him.

My dad is a driven career-man, aspiring to be the top educator in his field (which, after forty years, he has accomplished). Throughout my childhood, I treasured the little time we had together. He missed most of my Little League games, but I didn't care. He was my dad, and I thought he was the greatest one on Earth.

My child arrived just the other day,
He came to the world in the usual way.
But there were planes to catch, and bills to pay.
He learned to walk while I was away.
And he was talking 'fore I knew it, and as he grew,
He'd say, "I'm gonna be like you, Dad.
You know I'm gonna be like you".

And the cat's in the cradle and the silver spoon,
Little boy blue and the man in the moon.
"When you coming home, Dad?"
"I don't know when, but we'll get together then.
You know we'll have a good time then."

My son turned ten just the other day.
He said, "Thanks for the ball, Dad, come on let's play.
Can you teach me to throw?" I said, "Not today,
I got a lot to do." He said, "That's okay."
And he walked away, but his smile never dimmed.
And said, "I'm gonna be like him, yeah.
You know I'm gonna be like him."

So much of my childhood played out like this famous Harry Chapin song, *Cat's in the Cradle*. I was proud of my dad, and no matter how busy he was, I never gave up hope that soon he would have time to play with me.

As I got older and graduated college, career prospects started coming my way.

In 1997, I was offered an opportunity to relocate to the West Coast to represent a world class asset manager.

The race was on.

Within two years of moving to Seattle, I found myself with a "1K" membership with United Airlines, an honor bestowed to the company's exclusive 100,000 miles-a-year travelers. The counter clerks at the Hertz Gold desks up and down the West Coast knew my smile and my first name. I had built my own busy fast-paced career and, like my dad, had become a father myself.

Initially, my dad and mom would come to visit us religiously every six weeks. But as my miles in the sky increased and the demands of 21st century parenting took my weekends from one Little League game to the next, the visits became fewer. By the time I was thirty-five years old, my professional life had me in very high demand Monday through Friday, and as the father of two little boys, I was in high demand at home too.

I cherish what I learned from my father as I grew up watching him become the best in his business. He taught me a huge lesson in the value of following one's true purpose and developing the belief that you can transform the lives of many people. As a result, I have become a dedicated coach, both for my boys and for my clients. I was put on this Earth to challenge the status quo and teach others how to do the same. I'm obsessed with it.

Fortunately for me, I get to express my purpose through my daily interactions with my boys, teaching them about life and how to be a transformative figure themselves, and how to go completely counter to the culture. Most of this learning is happening through the great game of baseball. I don't care about the scoreboard--whether the team wins or loses in the eyes of our spectators. My boys have learned that going counter to the culture requires them to show up for baseball focused, grateful, confident, and ready to give it their all.

My schedule has become so full between my business and my boys, that I now find that I have less time to spend with my dad.

I've long since retired and my son's moved away.
I called him up just the other day.
I said, "I'd like to see you if you don't mind."
He said, "I'd love to, Dad, if I could find the time.
You see, my new job's a hassle and the kid's got the flu.
But it's sure nice talking to you, Dad.
It's been sure nice talking to you."
And as I hung up the phone, it occurred to me,
He'd grown up just like me.
My boy was just like me.

Every year, my dad, brother and I meet in Las Vegas for a wonderful long weekend.

We put aside our careers and our lives at home to just be with each other. We eat like royalty, have a few too many adult beverages, and play a little craps in our favorite casino. But the most important thing we do while we're together is talk. We talk about life, love, memories and dreams. It is three days each year I am very grateful to have. Although I often wonder what life would have been like if I had been able to spend more time with my dad growing up, I now realize that the time I did have with him was brilliantly perfect. And the time I have with him now is priceless.

My time with my dad for the past forty-three years has helped me figure out the kind of man I was meant to be. Our time together and the talks we've had helped me realize my true purpose: to challenge the status quo. It's also allowed me to shape the kind of relationships I now have with my two boys. And most important, it helped me feel a deep sense of gratitude for the time I did and currently do spend with my dad.

This, to me, is a huge measure of true wealth. I am a wealthy man.

Thank you, Dad, for sharing these very important lessons in building wealth. I love you more than you could ever imagine!

In 1970, Graham Nash wrote the song *Teach Your Children*. His struggles with his own father inspired him to produce a piece of music that evokes real emotion for almost everyone who hears it. Nash said about the song:

"The idea is that you write something so personal that every single person on the planet can relate to it. Once it's there on vinyl it unfolds, outwards, so that it applies to almost any situation."

In 2005, I found myself in a do-or-die financial firestorm. I had completely mismanaged my finances and had become the picture-perfect definition of the hypocritical, reckless spendthrift I had built a career lecturing others how *not* to be. It was the low point in my financial life.

I woke up every day in a cold sweat, embarrassed at my failures, living in constant fear that I would lose my job, lose my home, and lose my family. I hated myself.

But I eventually realized that this was bottom, and that I could make the difficult choices to right my financial ship. This was no small task, requiring the help of several advisors to help me stay accountable for making better choices. My impulsiveness was overwhelming, as was my self-loathing. To begin my journey forward required me to meet weekly with my therapist, Lani. She helped me learn to forgive myself for the disaster I had created around me. We'd spend weeks of couch time becoming aware of the triggers in my life that would encourage my impulsiveness to take over.

With time, growing awareness, and a great deal of discipline, our weekly talks became weekly celebrations of mini-achievements. This work translated incredibly well into the work I was doing with my financial advisors. I was able to reign in my spending and actually began to save. By learning how to forgive myself and by surrounding myself with the right people, I found myself in a much different financial position just six years after hitting bottom.

After escaping the clutches of corporate America in 2011, I chose to make it my purpose in life to challenge the status quo by teaching others how to own their financial mistakes, fix them, and pass those invaluable lessons learned onto their children. Whether your bills are paid in full at the end of every month, you stretched a little too far to buy a vacation home and a fancy car, or you have to do some hocus pocus to make ends meet, there's a good chance you have some less-than-perfect money habits.

These habits can have a profound effect on your children, just as mine did.

Despite what you may be thinking, your not-so-perfect money habits can serve an incredible purpose, and ultimately be one of the greatest gifts you ever give your children.

What are *your* bad money habits? What are your good ones? What money habits did you inherit from your parents, good or bad? What habits will you commit to changing for good, starting now?

Most young adults are entering the grown-up world without basic knowledge of how to balance a monthly budget or save for their future. Many are assuming massive debt in the form of car loans and student loans, and doing so without a clear vision of how to begin repayment of these debts one day. They are not being taught the basic principles of simple vs. compound interest, and how debt can cost them significantly over their lifetime. Public schools and universities have done a better job in increasing exposure to financial education; however, these efforts alone are largely unsuccessful and must be supported by good financial "home-schooling." The theories and opinions learned in a personal finance class cannot compare to the knowledge gained by witnessing and learning from the practical choices, mistakes, and real-life money decisions kids can see at home with their parents.

The potential for parents as teachers

From a very young age, children pay close attention to how money is treated in their home. Many parents are missing the opportunity to use these observations as teaching opportunities. Moms and dads I meet tell me they prefer not to say anything when there are struggles or disagreements about money, especially with things such as debt, paying for college, monthly budgeting and family income. They keep quiet because they believe it's best to protect their kids from their mistakes.

This can't be further from the truth, however. My personal experience, and my experience working with families and multi-generational wealth for the past twenty years, has taught me that parents who make significant money mistakes and involve their kids in the lessons learned from them can see a much greater impact on their kids making smart choices as they enter adulthood. So many studies and articles have been written on the topic. The strongest case for this argument is that the overwhelming majority of Millennials (those born between the mid-1980s and the early 2000s) despise debt. People might think their kids don't know about the $20,000 credit card balance Mom and Dad have, but they do know. Kids are very perceptive, and if Mom and Dad are secretly fighting about money, the kids know about it.

Children also know when their parents lack perfection. Practicing hypocrisy and lecturing them on how to make perfect choices about money will only drive them to more compulsive, destructive money behaviors. The fear I initially see from parents in speaking the truth is that their child will be their little copy-cat, making the same mistakes they have made. However, my experience has been quite the opposite. I have found that our kids and the kids of my clients are making much wiser choices with their money because of our honesty about our own mistakes, and the lessons we learned from those mistakes.

Some very basic things we can all teach our kids (based on mistakes I have made over the years) are:

- How to balance a checkbook or reconcile an online checking account.

- How to budget monthly for things like iDevices, new clothes, or fun with friends.

- How to value the true wealth created by investing their money in memory-making experiences with their friends rather the relentless pursuit of acquiring meaningless stuff.

- Giving back and allocating a portion of their money to a cause greater than themselves.

I recommend parents take a good honest look in the mirror.

Write down your money mistakes; past and present. Share these with your kids. It's an exercise with multiple benefits. First, it forces you to sit and become honest with yourself about where you may have mismanaged your finances. Awareness is the first step toward choosing a new path. Second, it allows you to become vulnerable and authentic in your relationship with your child, deepening their respect for you, and showing that a true leader owns his or her mistakes and works hard at fixing them. That's a priceless life lesson.

And finally, you can begin to prepare your kids for your estate and your legacy by teaching them to talk openly about financial blunders. Children need permission to make mistakes and develop the belief that they can become one of our most valuable assets.

Here are a few more habits to begin sharing with your children as you become aware of your lack of financial perfection and strive to become a better teacher:

Own your mistakes and devote yourself to fixing them

First things first: forgive yourself for not being perfect with money. If the best time to become a great steward of your money was twenty years ago, then the next best time is right now. Become aware of your mistakes, own them by writing them down, and be willing to learn how to fix them. If you don't know the best habits for using credit cards or how to make a household budget, seek professional help through a financial planner or tax planner, and learn with your child.

Create a family spending plan

Most families I meet make a good living and have substantial income, yet at the end of the month they often tell me they don't know where all the money went. Spending everything you make--or, even worse, spending more than you make--is a certain path toward insurmountable debt and poor lessons for the kids.

Consider setting a weekly or monthly family budget meeting. Sunday nights after dinner is a great time for everyone to sit down and review the family bills and upcoming expenses for the week. This way the kids can see exactly what it costs on a weekly basis to manage the household finances.

If you're like most parents, you probably hear things from your kids like, "Dad, why can't I buy a new iPhone for $800?"

If this is a question that has been asked in your family, an exercise in weekly family budget planning can provide the very quick and understandable answer that puts the kibosh on it, once and for all.

Be willing to admit when you make mistakes with your weekly budgeting by overspending on non-necessary items. Be open in discussing what you could do better as a family.

Save, no matter what

Not everyone believes they can afford to save. I encourage clients to read <u>The Richest Man in Babylon,</u> by George Clason, so they can learn the most important wealth building lesson of all: *the first person to get paid every pay period is <u>you</u>.*

Ten percent of your take-home income should go into savings before any bills get paid, even if this is as little as $10 per paycheck. It is critical to teach your kids the importance of investing in themselves and paying themselves before they pay anyone else. Ideally, your savings should include an emergency cash fund as well as a fund for your retirement, like a 401(k) or an IRA.

Protect your credit

Most everyone I know has debt: mortgage, car, student, and/or credit card debt. Debt has become part of the fiber of America. You as a parent must step up and show your children how important it is to properly manage and protect their credit. Even if you struggle to pay your outstanding debt, paying something is better than ignoring it.

If you are at a point where you have gotten in a little over your head with debt, involve your children in a discussion about how you got to this point and about handling your responsibilities going forward. Then call those you owe and make manageable payment arrangements with a timetable of when your debt will be paid off. It's an incredible lesson to teach your kids: sometimes we just have to deal with cleaning up financial mistakes, no matter how hard it is.

Agree to disagree

Disagreements about money can be some of the most damaging dynamics in a family environment. I meet families all the time who have different priorities when it comes to money. In 2013, Fidelity Corporation conducted a study about couples being on the same page about finances[1]. Their study concluded that 8 out of 10 couples believed they were in synch, when in fact they had very different priorities and beliefs when it came to money and how it should be used.

It's no wonder so many families battle over financial issues, but it doesn't have to be that way. In my private wealth management practice, I encourage families to sit and have discussions about differing views on money. Where do we agree? Where do we struggle to agree? Can we truly listen to one another's beliefs and work to support one another despite our differences?

This is not an easy exercise, and families that have a hard time tackling it should seek professional help. This is some of the most important work we do in our business. We work with families to help them establish agreements about money, especially in the areas where there is much disagreement. Family fights about finances that are not resolved are some of the most harmful interactions that can happen, especially in the presence of the kids.

I've shared my mistakes with my children, and their financial habits are better because of them. My oldest son is saving his money to buy his first car in a little over a year, and he's already contemplating the best ways to save for and pay for his college education. My younger son saves his money for Calvin and Hobbes books; nonetheless, he's learned an important lesson in valuing money and what it can buy you if you treat it with respect.

As parents, there's nothing we want more than for our children to do better than we have in life. Helping them learn from our mistakes is a big part of the process.

You, who are on the road, must have a code that you can live by.
And so become yourself, because the past is just a goodbye.
Teach your children well. Their father's hell did slowly go by.
And feed them on your dreams. The one they pick's, the one
you'll know by.

Don't you ever ask them why? If they told you, you would cry.
So just look at them and sigh.
And know they love you.

And you of tender years can't know the fears that your elders
grew by.

And so please help them with your youth. They seek the truth
before they can die.

Teach your parents well. Their children's hell will slowly go by.
And feed them on your dreams. The one they pick's, the one
you'll know by.

Don't you ever ask them why? If they told you, you would cry.
So just look at them and sigh.
And know they love you.

"Teach Your Children"
By Graham Nash
Crosby, Stills & Nash

FIND YOUR SWEET SPOT

UNREALISTIC EXPECTATIONS **vs.** **REALISTIC** EXPECTATIONS

EXPECTATIONS

SOUR

REALITY

EXPECTATIONS

SWEET

REALITY

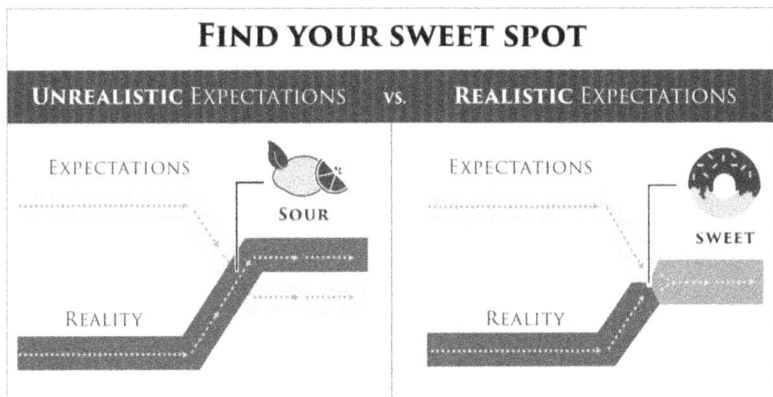

Are you constantly irritated by a tardy co-worker? Are your teenage kids driving you nuts because they never seem to pick up after themselves? Does it bother you that your boss is nit-picky about the stupidest things? Are you unsatisfied with the returns you get on your 401(k) compared to everyone you talk to?

If you answered yes to any of these questions, you may have some unrealistic expectations.

If you find yourself feeling regularly annoyed with others failing to meet your expectations, you have two choices: continue to expect them to change their behavior, and keep on being annoyed when they don't; or learn how to properly adjust your expectations and eliminate your daily torment. Neither choice is easy. However, experience has taught me one option will leave you feeling much less angst on a day-to-day basis than the other.

I know what you're thinking. How can this guy expect me to accept anything less than excellence in those around me? It's not my job to change…it's theirs!

I get it. But demanding excellence and setting realistic expectations are mutually exclusive things. They do not necessarily go hand in hand.

Let me give you an example.

I demand excellence out of everyone I hire. I recently hired a Director of Operations; someone I know can perform with the excellence I expect. The criteria for how I found, and then hired this individual, are the basis for creating the expectation that she would be nothing less than excellent.

I'll come back to this example shortly to show you why this is a reasonable expectation.

Are you ready to establish more realistic expectations? Are you ready to do away with a big part of your daily frustration? Here are three tips to consider when setting expectations.

Tip 1: Control Factor

The first test in determining if an expectation is realistic is to look at how much control you have over the matter at hand.

Can you control the return on your 401(k)? Can you make your co-worker be on time for team meetings? Can you make your teenager pick up his mess? The answer to these questions is a resounding "no." I guess you could withhold allowance to force your teenager into cleaning up after himself, but he can still choose not to do it despite the consequences, right?

To have an expectation based on something entirely outside your control only sets you up for frustration and letdown. Expecting your 401(k) to grow by 20% every year, or expecting your kids to pick up after themselves, is as realistic as expecting to see sunshine and 80-degree weather every day in Seattle. The bottom line is that if you have little to no control over the outcome you expect, you have set an *unreasonable* expectation.

Tip 2: The History Test

Let's pick on my teenage son again.

For fourteen of his fifteen years on Earth, I lived with constant frustration, especially during the middle school years. He could never seem to keep his room clean. He never seemed to turn his homework in on time. And he always copped an attitude when I would nag him about either or both. Our father/son relationship was deteriorating rapidly until someone I trust asked me a magical question that woke me up to my reality as a parent of a teenager.

My therapist Lani said, "Why do you expect your son to clean his room and handle his schoolwork when he never has before?"

That was the moment I chose not to expect that my son's room would be clean or his homework would be turned in on time. The byproduct of eliminating this expectation is that when he does clean his room or meet schoolwork deadlines, I am pleasantly surprised and I shower him with praise. This happens a lot more since abolishing my expectations.

Coincidence?

Not only is this a positive for my son, it has also been a positive for our relationship. We used to spend entire weekends angry at each other. He was frustrated at himself for being mindless with his schoolwork, and I was mad at him for it. Now, we enjoy our weekends and my son has actually found the motivation to be more mindful of his cleanliness around the house. Even more important, he is turning in his work and getting all As and Bs. The effect this modification of my expectations has had on the overall happiness in our family is profound.

The takeaway is this: if history tells you one thing, expecting a different outcome in the future is unrealistic.

Tip 3: Stop Staring at the Horizon

Although we have discussed mostly setting realistic expectations for others, doing this can only happen if you set realistic expectations for yourself.

Do you feel unhappy with your professional progress? Do you feel like you should be further along in your career? Do you feel frustrated with the lack of retirement savings you have accumulated? Do you get mad at yourself when you're late for a meeting?

I have met many people in my life, and I have yet to come across the perfect person.

Yet so many people I know expect perfection of themselves. You might be one of them. You might say you don't, but you do.

When was the last time you made a mistake and were okay with it? *Really* okay with it? If you're like most people I meet, you kick yourself inwardly and then find yourself yelling at your kids an hour later for doing the same thing.

Be honest. I've been there and I know you have too.

How do we set realistic expectations for ourselves? We often look at the horizon and compare where we think we should be to where we are now, whether it is at work, in our retirement savings, in our overall happiness in life.

But the horizon is not a realistic place to set expectations, because you can never reach it. Rather, we should spend more time looking at history (remember Tip 2) to see how far we have actually come. You will be amazed at your progress when you take that historical perspective, instead of feeling constant disappointment over failing to meet your own expectations by looking at a far and distant horizon.

Repeat after me: "I give myself permission to make mistakes."

Say this over and over. Setting realistic expectations for others starts with setting them for you.

Let's get back to my new hire and why I can expect excellence.

First, I get to choose whom I hire. Control factor: check!

Second, I have worked closely with this person for ten years in volunteer capacities. After watching her work ethic, her attention to detail and her belief that perfect is better than done, I knew she was the right fit for my firm. History test: check!

Despite expecting excellence, I also know there will be mistakes along the way. Acknowledging this still allows me to believe in and expect excellence in those I choose to have around me.

I believe it's okay to make mistakes, as long as you own them and fix them. Allow yourself to be imperfect and set reasonable expectations for yourself. *Really*. Once you have done this, you will be equipped with the tips in this chapter to set realistic expectations for others. The benefit to you will be much more peace and much less irritation in your everyday life. I promise!

(By the way, I have no expectation that you will actually change your expectations of yourself and others!)

True leadership in today's world requires new thinking.

Leadership over the past twenty-five years has established a society that has surrendered to mediocrity. Despite the occasional blasphemy expressed in social media, most people are not willing to do what it takes to see our society reverse course. We have become comfortable with the status quo. Very few have truly risen up to say "good enough" is not good enough.

Nowhere is this more true than in the financial services industry.

I am very proud to be part of the new generation of leaders willing to go counter to the culture. At our firm, we are obsessed with challenging the status quo and transforming the way people save for retirement, simply because the current system is okay with mediocrity. That system caters to a select few, high-net-worth individuals—the "One Percent Club." The advice made available to the rest of us is completely riddled with conflicts of interest, benefitting the biggest brokerage firms on Wall Street and the mutual fund industry much more than the investors they are supposed to serve.

Another true leader, one of the few who has decided to go counter to the culture, is Dan Price, CEO of Gravity Payments in Seattle, Washington. Mr. Price recently surprised his 120-person staff by announcing that within the next three years, his company will be implementing a new minimum wage policy: $70,000 annual salaries. Price feels that the growing pay discrepancy between workers and CEOs is getting out of hand. He also believes that when employees don't worry about money, they are more productive at work and raise the success level of the overall organization.

To accomplish this goal of eliminating financial stress for employees and raising the minimum pay bar as high as he has, this CEO will have to make some substantial adjustments to his own compensation package. To this end, Price announced that he will be lowering his compensation to the $70,000-a-year mark until profitability in his company increases substantially as a result of this new direction.

Dan Price is finished following the prevailing style of leadership of executives across America. He has adopted a *servant leadership* approach to running a business: a style that is devoted to serving his employees and creating an atmosphere of complete buy-in and belief in the purpose of the organization. Equitable compensation is a huge component of servant leadership, and Price has shown that he is committed to going counter to the culture.

HERZBERG'S MOTIVATIONAL FACTORS THEORY

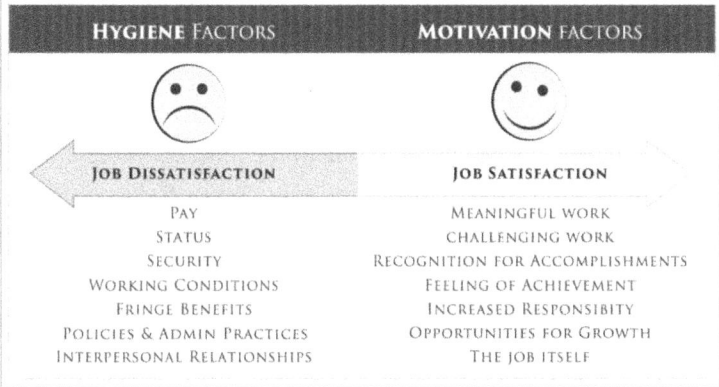

HYGIENE Factors	MOTIVATION Factors
JOB DISSATISFACTION	JOB SATISFACTION
PAY	MEANINGFUL WORK
STATUS	CHALLENGING WORK
SECURITY	RECOGNITION FOR ACCOMPLISHMENTS
WORKING CONDITIONS	FEELING OF ACHIEVEMENT
FRINGE BENEFITS	INCREASED RESPONSIBITY
POLICIES & ADMIN PRACTICES	OPPORTUNITIES FOR GROWTH
INTERPERSONAL RELATIONSHIPS	THE JOB ITSELF

HERZBERG'S TWO-FACTOR THEORY STATES THAT CERTAIN FACTORS CAUSE JOB SATISFACTION, AND A SEPARATE SET OF FACTORS CAUSE DISSATISFACTION. ALTHOUGH HERZBERG IS MOST NOTED FOR HIS FAMOUS 'HYGIENE' AND MOTIVATIONAL FACTORS THEORY, HE WAS ESSENTIALLY CONCERNED WITH PEOPLE'S WELL-BEING AT WORK.

Rarely will I try to forecast anything, especially market returns or matters related to economics. I will however, put a little reputational risk on the line by predicting the success of Gravity Payments. I have little doubt that this organization will attract the kind of people who want to be part of something much greater than mediocrity, the kind of people who are "in it to win it" because they want to be part of a culture and a team that means more than just making money. This is certainly not the last time we will be reading about Mr. Price and his organization. I suspect we will see great success from this team, and I will certainly not be surprised to see Gravity Payments one day being one of the most profitable employers in the Pacific Northwest, if not the entire country.

We know the current economic structure in our country is broken, thanks to mediocre leadership. From executive pay to minimum wage to entitlements to retirement planning, it's a mess, and as a society we must take responsibility for the leaders we have tolerated for so long.

According to the *BBC News*, a great modern-day failure in business leadership happened at one of the most revered companies of all time: Microsoft. In 2000, Steve Balmer was handed a legacy by Microsoft founder, Bill Gates. Since taking over the company, Mr. Balmer and his C-suite executive team have missed one opportunity after another. They have been playing catch-up for nearly fifteen years as technology has zipped right past them in areas such as mobile devices, social media, and live streaming. The company has continued to maintain a vertical stack ranking structure that has deeply affected Microsoft's culture and their ability to attract and retain talent. The top performers get bonuses and the bottom performers lose their jobs. This has significantly reduced collaboration within the organization. The culture has also reinforced a big-company mentality to protect the company's monopoly position at the expense of taking sizeable risks to create and innovate.

We are attacking the problem of mediocre leadership by constantly challenging the status quo. We are helping millions of workers save for retirement the right way—a new way that's easy to understand and implement. It's very affordable, and most important, it is completely free from conflict of interest. Hopefully we will begin to see more and more businesses like our firm and Gravity Payments emerge, whose leaders are willing to go counter to the culture so that the now-defunct great American dream can once again be reborn for this generation of American workers.

Is there something wrong when the executives of a company are rewarded for sending 20,000 people to the unemployment lines? Or is that an acceptable part of doing business?

On April 17, 2015, the oil giant Schlumberger announced that it was slashing 11,000 more jobs as oil price declines were devastating company profits. That was after letting go of 9,000 people already. As a result of the announcement, the stock price of Schlumberger rallied, up more than 1% the day's trading.

From a business perspective, I get the decision to cut those jobs. Less overhead, or cost of doing business, means stronger profitability. That translates to a more "valuable" company. Again, I get it. It gives me flashbacks to my sophomore microeconomics class at Albany State University.

But a stronger sense of humanness inside of me says that cutting all those people out is simply "bass-ackwards". It just stinks. By increasing value by 1%, Schlumberger's largest shareholders--namely its top executives, board of directors, hedge fund managers, and large mutual fund companies—were financially rewarded by turning the lives of 20,000 workers upside down. That's 20,000 people who had families that depended on them to put food on their table, a roof over their heads, clothes on their backs, and the opportunity for an education. That's 20,000 people who were integral to the company's success. Yet they were taken out back and shot in the head for the purpose of greater profit.

In the last chapter, I wrote about Dan Price, CEO of Gravity Payments in Seattle, Washington, who announced that he was cutting his pay as CEO to bring his company's minimum wage up to $70,000 per year. Not only is he preserving jobs, Mr. Price is setting his company up to expand at the cost of short-term profitability. The long-term value of what Gravity will provide society is tremendous, as the company develops a culture of employees who believe they belong to something very special.

Despite the 29% decline in profit, Schlumberger was still able to squeak out a paltry *ten billion dollars* in 1st quarter revenue in 2015. Any chance that CEO Paal Kibsgaard considered a reduction in his compensation, similar to Dan Price's, for the sake of his employees?

Not likely.

Schlumberger was not alone. The slide in oil prices around this time cost nearly 200,000 people their jobs in the oil industry. Schlumberger just happened to be my target because they were the unlucky ones in the news that day. But am I to expect that the executive team at Schlumberger, and their peers in big oil, believe that the global demand for energy will continue to slide forever, so much so that it's worth destroying the families of 200,000 workers?

At the rate of population growth across the world and with advances in technology, we are just getting started when it comes to global energy demand. India, with 1.2 billion people, is about to top the 1.3 billion person population in China. Both countries are seeing incredible growth in the middle class, where energy demands are soaring. In the US, the Millennial generation is the first to outnumber baby boomers, creating a greater demand for energy here at home. And as our global climate continues to change and we experience much more extreme weather and temperatures, the overall demand for heat and air conditioning will undoubtedly continue to expand. Yet Schlumberger placed a greater value on one quarter's profits than on positioning itself as an innovator to meet future energy needs.

This story points out what I find wrong with our current reward system in corporate America. Instead of killing the livelihoods of thousands of families, why not reinvent roles within the oil companies, to position themselves as true leaders in providing for future needs for global energy?

Well, Mr. Price, I guess it's up to us hopeless idealists to try and effect change.

8 OUT OF 10 ENTREPRENEURS WHO START A BUSINESS
FAIL WITHIN THE FIRST 18 MONTHS

"I wanna be a millionaire, so friggin' bad...."

Bruno Mars sang it and millions of Millennials rallied as if this were their new generational battle cry. For most of the under-forty crowd, Bruno's idea seems pretty far-fetched. But the reality of Millennials becoming millionaires is much more likely than for any previous generation.

Why? Simply put, because they have time.

There are two paths Millennials can take to become millionaires: the private markets and the public markets. The private markets will certainly get you there quicker, but success in the private market comes with substantial risk, and failure is frequent. When I refer to the private markets, I'm talking about starting your own business with a profitable, sustainable model that one day is worth a lot of money in someone's eyes. The upside can be huge.

The youngest billionaire on the planet is Facebook's own Mark Zuckerberg, who created the world's most famous social media site from his Harvard dorm room at twenty years old.

However, the route for most is not that of Mr. Zuckerberg. It's a grueling path of starting and managing a business, hiring and firing people, developing a loyal customer base, growing that customer base, creating balance between top-line growth and bottom-line management, and one day selling that business to a private equity firm--or a large competitor who wants to take you out, hopefully for a price that is a much greater than your investment.

The statistical probability of starting a business on a $20,000 loan from your dad and turning into a multimillion-dollar enterprise is not good. According to Bloomberg, 8 out of 10 entrepreneurs who start a business fail within the first eighteen months.

With an 80% failure rate in the private markets, the public markets seem a bit more in favor of living the dream in Bruno Mars' song. It will take time and whole lot of patience, but a Millennial who can exhibit a bit of discipline should have a high probability of reaching that millionaire status during his or her lifetime.

The public markets path is the traditional path of employment and the ability to save a portion of your paycheck every month in a 401(k) or other company-sponsored retirement plan. The challenge for most then becomes reaching that million-dollar net-worth mark. There a few tips I've learned on my journey of failures and successes (I reached the million-dollar savings mark at age 38. My business partner did it by 31):

TIP #1:
Start young and believe in magic
(the magic of compound interest)

T+CI= ChaChing.

It's my favorite mathematical formula: time plus compound interest equals a whole bunch of money. It's the most effective formula for building wealth in the public markets. The reason is based on a simple rule called "The Rule of 72." It works like this:

THE RULE OF 72

72/your rate of return = number of years to double your money

x **10%** = **2X**
RATE OF RETURN   YOUR MONEY

Every 7.2 years, you will double your money.

72 DIVIDED BY YOUR RATE OF RETURN = NUMBER OF YEARS TO DOUBLE YOUR MONEY

If you earn a 10% rate of return over time (the market average since 1926 is approximately 10%), you can expect to double your money every 7.2 years. If you are more conservative than the stock market (it takes quite a strong stomach to ride the roller coaster of the market up and down) and you play a bit more defense with your money, a target return of 7.2% would mean your money doubles every ten years. That means every dollar you invest at age 25 will be worth $16 at retirement.

TIP #2:
Have a disciplined strategy that can play offense and defense.

Whether you work with an advisor or develop your game plan on your own, it's critical to have a strategy that you can follow based on the goals you have set for yourself.

Wall Street brokerage firms and the big mutual fund companies have been promoting a strategy called "buy and hold" for decades. It's a misguided approach that benefits the big firms more than it benefits you, the investor. The big firms want to see you stay fully invested in stocks and bonds at all times. They can't earn a fee if you're not. The problem with staying fully invested at all times is that you are forced to ride the market waves up *and* down, and you're left hoping it all works out one day when you need your savings.

Anyone planning retirement around 2008-2009 who took the advice of the big Wall Street brokerage firms saw 30-60% of their retirement savings vanish in less than a year. The average "buy and hold" investor who had saved $1,000,000 in a 401(k) saw $300,000-$600,000 of that savings flushed down the toilet. Since 84% of all 401(k) assets are invested in target series funds (according to Fidelity Inc.), the majority of 401(k) savers saw these results firsthand in 2008-2009. The Fidelity 2020 Fund was down over 35% in 2008, which translates to a $350,000 loss for a retirement saver with a $1 million 401(k) plan.

Imagine if that happened a year or two before you planned to retire. Ouch!

There's an old saying in sports that "offense wins ballgames, but defense wins championships."

Having an all-offense strategy with your 401(k) will definitely yield some good years. But without playing some defense during the more difficult bear market years, you could leave yourself in shambles when you need your 401(k) the most.

There are a few firms out there that are willing to counter the Wall Street brokerage firm culture of "buy and hold." My firm is one of them. We believe in protecting 401(k) savings by implementing a strategy that plays offense *and* defense.

TIP #3:
Get to know your new best friend, Vol A. Tility.

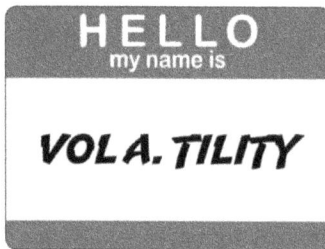

Despite playing offense and defense, you will always experience some volatility in your 401(k). This is nothing to be afraid of. In fact, a moderate amount of volatility can become your new best friend if you know how to use it right.

If you are investing the same amount each paycheck, you will accumulate more shares when prices drop and fewer shares when prices go up. Here's a simple example of why this is so powerful. Let's say you invest $100 each pay period into Fund XYZ. For this pay period Fund XYZ is at $10 per share. That means you buy ten shares. Imagine if, by the next pay period, Fund XYZ has fallen to $5 per share. Yes, your original shares just got cut in half, but you will now purchase twenty shares for the same $100. At the next pay period, Fund XYZ rebounds back to $10 per share and you buy ten more. Here's what that looks like:

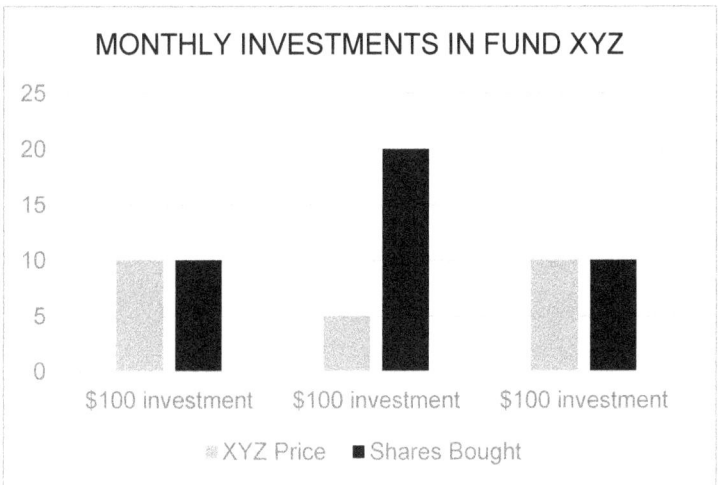

MONTHLY INVESTMENTS IN FUND XYZ

Let's now analyze the outcome of the last three months of investing in Fund XYZ.

- Amount Invested = $300
- Total Shares Purchased = 40
- XYZ Price After Month 3 = $10 per share
- Total Investment Value = $400

- Investment Gain (or loss) = +33%

Interestingly enough, the return of Fund XYZ over that time period is 0% because it started at $10 and ended at $10. But because you invested monthly throughout the three months, your personal return was 33%.

Not bad, right?

This strategy is the best way to accumulate shares over long periods of time and take advantage of some moderate volatility. As you accumulate more shares, it's critical to remember our second tip for success--playing defense.

TIP #4:
Believe in the stock market.

Despite all that we may read about the risks of investing in the stock market, no asset on Earth has delivered the consistent returns that the stock market has over the past century. With interest rates at historical lows, the best yield on your money can often come from the dividends paid by big corporations to their stock holders.

CDs historically have been considered a much safer option than the stock market. However, if we remember the Rule of 72, a CD paying 1% will take 72 years to double in value (that's assuming you can still find a CD paying a whole 1%). Investing in real estate can often be appealing as well, as this is a hard asset that you can touch and feel. The problem you run into with investing your retirement savings in real estate is that it comes with the same risks as the stock market, and then some. Not only can prices fluctuate wildly, but you also encounter what's called liquidity risk: the ability to access your money when you need it. Selling a piece of your real estate portfolio to buy groceries can be a challenge but one that could happen in a bad real estate market.

A strategy that exposes your savings to the stock market or portions of the stock market is the most efficient way to take advantage of all of the tips we recommend. These are the tips I found to be most useful in helping me accumulate my million-dollar savings account. By age 38, I had accumulated enough money to walk away from corporate America and put it into building my own business and creating jobs for others in my community.

No, I don't drive an expensive car or live in a big fancy house. I own a business that helps a lot of people. Although it's a bit different than what Bruno Mars sings about, that's why I wanted to be a millionaire, so friggin' bad!

Whether graduating high school or college, many young adults enter the full-time work force for the first time when they finish their formal education. During those initial few months facing the reality of life after school, choices are made that kick off a life-long journey of important financial decisions.

It all starts with finding that first full-time job and choosing the right mix of corporate benefits like health insurance, disability insurance, group life insurance, and setting up a 401(k). Next comes purchasing a car, making a down payment on a first home, getting married and having kids, and ultimately saving for college so your kids can earn a degree of their own.

How does one even start down this path of adulthood and begin to tackle these major financial decisions?

Currently, the job market is the best it has been since before the 2008 financial crisis. So it all starts with landing full-time employment as soon as possible after graduation. Once that job is secure, there are a few simple tips to help graduates stand on their own two feet and avoid the necessity of tapping the Bank of Mom and Dad.

Tip #1:
Treat your personal balance sheet like a business

I hate to state the obvious, but it never hurts to remind people to spend less than they earn. It's a critical habit to start now. Simply put, run your personal balance sheet like you are a business. A business cannot be successful if it spends more than it earns. Neither can an individual.

Creating a business-like balance sheet for your personal finances is not as difficult as you might think. Start with writing down how much you earn (gross wages) on a blank sheet of paper. Below your gross wages, subtract 10%. That amount will be placed into an inaccessible savings account. For example, if you earn $5,000 per month, or $2,500 per bi-monthly paycheck, set aside $250 per paycheck into savings ($500 per month). We will call this account your "profit" account. It's a simple way to make sure you pay yourself before you pay anyone else.

Next, account for payroll deductions like federal and state income taxes, FICA (Social Security and Medicare), health insurance, and 401(k) contributions. Since these are automatically done for you, simply record them on your balance sheet directly under your 10% profit distribution. After you have accounted for these initial deductions from your gross income, you now have a remaining balance that can be used to cover your monthly expenses.

Here's the most important part of running your personal finances like a business: *do not spend more than you have in this remaining balance*.

Your finished balance sheet should look something like this:

Total Monthly Income	$5,000
Profit Distribution	$500
Emergency Fund	$500
Taxes	$750
FICA	$250
Health Insurance	$250
401k	$500
Remaining Balance For Expenses	$2,250

The balance of $2,250 is now what you have to manage your monthly expenses, including rent, utilities, car payments, cell phone bills, food, and entertaining.

I'll explain the methodology behind this type of personal balance sheet in the next several tips.

Tip #2:
Pay yourself first

With graduation from school in the rear view mirror, learning and growing financially has really just begun.

Rule number one is to make sure you budget every month to pay yourself first, as you saw in the balance sheet example in Tip #1. Before rent, car payments, utility bills, or cell phone bills, set aside 10% of your gross paycheck in a savings account that is dedicated toward helping you become a better "you."

This money is not for a new tattoo or a big-screen TV. It could be, however, for taking an online graduate class to help you develop greater knowledge in your field of work; it could be for a gym membership to stay in top physical and mental shape for becoming a top performer; it could be money set aside for a few new work outfits so you look your best.

Regardless of how you choose to invest in "you," always remember that *you are your own greatest asset*. You must learn to set aside funds to help you continue to improve your skills, your health, your image and your opportunities.

Tip #3:
Create your rainy day fund

After setting aside 10% to invest in your future "you," your next 10% must be deducted for a rainy day or emergency fund.

A recent study by Bankrate.com showed more than 60% of Americans have virtually no savings set aside in an emergency fund. As you take on more and more financial obligations (such as car payment, mortgage, and student loan debt), the risk of running into unexpected financial troubles increases. To protect yourself from the inevitable, create another savings account, separate from your "pay yourself first" account, that allows you to build a cash cushion for the unexpected.

Before you even consider purchasing your first home, it is wise to have at least three months of salary set aside for emergencies if you're single, six months of salary if you're married with children. By saving another 10% of your income every month, you'll be able to accumulate a few months of salary before you know it.

Tip #4:
Buy health insurance

Many young and healthy workers are tempted to skip enrolling in a health insurance plan as a way to pocket more of their paychecks.

Consider health insurance one more investment in you. Remember, you are your most important asset. Health insurance for a young, healthy worker is very cheap compared to basic medical care. One day in the emergency room can cost tens of thousands of dollars. A recent study estimates that 18% to 26% of personal bankruptcies are related to medical debts, so it's critical to budget for insurance so you can avoid adding to that horrifying statistic.

Tip #5:
Enroll in a 401(k) or contribute to a Roth IRA

Most 18 to 25-year-olds have difficulty thinking about an obligation forty days from now, let alone plan for a retirement forty years in the future. But the sooner young people start saving for retirement, the better off they'll be come retirement.

Most employers offer some sort of pre-tax savings tool to help you set the groundwork for a secure retirement; this is usually called a 401(k), 403(b), or 457 deferred-comp plan. Even if you do not have this benefit at work, you can contribute up to

$5,500 per year into an individual retirement account (IRA), or, even better, a Roth IRA.

The benefit of a Roth IRA over a traditional IRA is that although both allow you defer paying taxes on your growth until retirement, a Roth IRA allows you to take money out for retirement completely tax-free.

It's important to remember that whatever you save in a 401(k) or IRA is meant for your retirement and should not be considered savings for a rainy day. Anything you withdraw from these accounts prior to age 59 ½ will be taxed heavily (ordinary income tax) as well as assessed a premature withdrawal penalty tax of 10%.

So start early and consider retirement savings a gift from your younger self to your older self. Despite the temptation to ignore retirement until you get much older, starting now makes a huge difference.

Let's look at an example.

Allison and John are both 25 and make the same income. Allison decides to begin saving for retirement, and starts funding her 401(k) with $458 per month ($5,500 per year) with pre-tax money. At age 40, after 15 years of contributions, Allison chooses to stop.

John decides to delay saving for retirement until he feels a bit more financially secure. At age 40, he starts funding his 401(k) with the same amount as Allison--$458 per month--until he retires at age 65.

- Allison's 15 years of contributing $5,500 per year (from age 25 to 40), will total $82,500 contributed.

- John's 25 years of contributing $5,500 per year (from age 40 to 65), will total $137,500 contributed.

Assuming an 8% average annual rate of return, Allison will have $1,066,520 accumulated in her 401(k) by the time she reaches age 65. But by the time John turns 65, he will have only $419,298 in his 401(k).

That's a huge difference! Even though Allison will fund her 401(k) at $5,500 per year and stop when she turns 40, she will have already accumulated $155,731 in her account, which will earn an average annual rate of return of 8% per year through age 65. With just the earnings on her 401(k) balance, and no additional contributions to the plan for 25 years, Allison's retirement nest egg will be nearly $600,000 greater than John's.

John will have contributed more to his 401(k) than Allison, even though Allison still ends up with far more money.

In addition to starting early, keep in mind that many employers also offer a 401(k) "match." This means that they will match a certain percentage of your contributions to the plan. Most often, companies match up to 3-6% of your income. So if you make $50,000 and contribute 10% ($5,000) of your income to your 401(k), your company could potentially add as much as another $5,000 a year on your behalf.

By not contributing the minimum amount to get a potential employer match, you're throwing away the opportunity to earn free retirement money.

So start saving at least 6% of your paycheck every pay period in your 401(k)--I recommend 10%--and continue to increase your percentage every year until you hit the maximum amount you can save ($18,500 in 2015-2016).

Tip #7:
Start building credit

Learning how to use credit at a young age is an important life skill. Although you should never spend more than you make, learning the proper way to handle credit is a key component to running your personal balance sheet like a successful business.

Begin by opening up a credit card at your local bank with a modest spending limit. Make a few purchases each month and pay off the bill in full. This will help build credit and good borrowing habits, both of which you will need to establish by the time you are ready to buy your first home.

It's like building muscle memory as an athlete. Once you create the discipline to pay your credit card bill every month, it becomes a life-long habit that simply happens automatically. Building this muscle starts by remembering that a credit card is not a license to buy what you cannot afford today. You must learn the discipline of paying your balances off every month and budgeting properly. To pay interest on an expensive dinner or new watch is not a smart use of your capital or your credit.

This may sound like a lecture you have heard before, titled "Do as I Say, Not as I Do." Well, it is. I tell you this from my own personal pain…the incredible pain of regret. By the time I was thirty years old, I had accrued over $100,000 in credit card and consumer debt. What I had to show for all of that wasted spending was very little. Sure, I owned two Rolex watches and a nice German car. But most of the time, the watches sat on my night table collecting dust, and by the time the car was paid for, it ran like an old jalopy.

The mountain of credit card debt left me with very little memory of the fancy dinners or new outfits I had acquired. There was no greater feeling of failure than to have reached the pinnacle of my professional career, only to realize I had maxed out all of my available credit by purchasing meaningless stuff, and then be left with no purchasing power to manage a family crisis (or even put gas in my car).

Tip #8:
Spend Meaningfully

Despite all of these money-saving tips I've provided, the idea of spending some money is okay. After all, this is your 20s we're talking about, and this time of life should be fun. But at the risk of sounding a bit too philosophical, is a new iPhone every year or $15 a day in lattes really what you want to remember most about life after college?

If you've done a good job creating a solid financial budget, there's nothing wrong with spending some money. Just consider using it on things that will create great life-long memories of the people and places than matter the most to you. A weekly dinner out with good friends, a backpacking trip through Europe with your old college roommate, a cross-country drive with your BFF…these are all things that you will look back on as memories worth the money spent.

Binge on experiences, and not gadgets that will be obsolete in a year.

A simple guide for spending is to follow the 10-10-10 rule. It basically goes like this: how will you feel about a purchase or an expense in ten weeks, ten months, and ten years? If the expense will be meaningless in ten weeks, skip it; you can certainly live without it. If the purchase will have a lasting effect in ten weeks but won't roll your socks up and down in ten months, consider delaying it until you come across some extra money. If the expense will still have you talking about it ten years from now, *go for it* without hesitation.

Tip #9:
Accept that you do not know everything

Ask for help when you're unsure...and I'm not talking about asking Siri.

Ask your dad about his first car purchase, and then ask for his advice. Ask your friends what they pay for rent. Ask your mom for an introduction to her financial advisor to help you with your 401(k) options. Get an introduction to a trusted accountant to talk about your taxes.

You have grown up in a digital age where everything you wanted to know was in the palm of your hand, thanks to Google. But it's important to know that there are no universal truths to money and saving for the future. What may be good advice for your college roommate may not be good advice for you. There is no online digital substitution for in-person, custom advice, and the help is out there for you.

All you need to do is recognize you don't have all the answers, and ask for help.

PART III:

BUILDING AND PROTECTING WEALTH

Introduction

It was a calm, cool Saturday morning as the sun came up over Clover Valley. I was driving down the private road to the entrance of my local neighborhood golf course. Three friends and I had the sunrise tee time--something we had been looking forward to for months. Normally dads like us don't get to play golf on Saturday mornings; they're usually spent prepping baseball fields for an entire day of Little League games. This was our lucky weekend off.

As I drove past a very familiar Chevy Malibu, I saw my good friend and dentist, Steve, crouched behind his sedan (in an obvious attempt to hide from the world), sucking on a Marlboro Lite like it was nectar of the gods.

A little smile came across my face. This was going to be fun.

Despite Steve's constant chastising of me over the years for my tobacco habits, there he was at 6 AM on a Saturday, closet-smoking a mile away from his house.

"What the hell are you doing?" I shouted with a huge grin on my face.

He was obviously startled.

"Please don't tell anyone. I feel like such a hypocrite," he said.

I chuckled. I let him off the hook too easily, in hindsight.

"Hey man, I wrote the book on *Do as I Say, Not as I Do*. So your secret is safe with me. Just stop busting my stones about my occasional social cigarette at the bar or infrequent wad of chew on the baseball field."

He laughed in relief and continued his secret morning nicotine binge.

That morning proved to me that *knowing* the right thing and *doing* the right thing don't always wind up together in harmonious matrimony.

This section of the book is about the "how to" of building the financial security component of true wealth. Despite being a financial mess myself at times, two decades in my industry have helped me acquire quite a bit of knowledge on how to save and invest successfully. I haven't always followed my own advice, but these are ideas that work.

Have you ever asked yourself questions like: How do I even begin to rebuild my wealth? Or begin building it for the first time? What mistakes am I okay making along the way? What mistakes do I need to avoid at all costs?

Part II will start helping you discover answers to these very questions. Even if you find yourself still unsure after reading this section, you will at least have the foundation of knowledge to know where to look for answers to your remaining questions.

Not every chapter is meant for every reader. Some chapters will be relevant to you now, and others may be more relevant down the road or for someone else you know.

Did you know that there is a simple formula, something you likely learned in middle school, for calculating your future wealth potential?

It all starts with a little temptation and curiosity.

Have you ever wondered how long it would take to double your money in a 401(k) or an IRA? Believe it or not, you can figure it out pretty easily; hence the middle school math reference. I briefly mentioned this formula a couple chapters ago, but it's well worth repeating in much more detail.

According to the Stern School of Business at New York University[2], since 1928, stocks have averaged about 11% return per year; bonds have averaged about 5% per year, and cash has averaged about 1% per year, although according to Bankrate.com[3], today's average money market rate in America is 0.09%. *It's important to know that these are long-term averages, and rarely do these investments actually return their exact average in any given year.* Earning these average returns over time requires patience and understanding that in any given year, your actual return could fluctuate considerably above or below the average long-term return quoted above.

In fact, the stock market has only returned its average (between 10-11%) *three times* since 1928 (10.81% in 1968, 9.97% in 1993, and 10.74% in 2004). That's only three out of 87 years! The remaining 84 years have delivered returns much greater or much less than that 10-11% average.

Why is this information so important to calculating one's future wealth? It all boils down to a simple formula called "The Rule of 72." The Rule of 72 is a mathematical certainty that says if you take 72 and divide it by your annual average return, your answer will yield exactly how long it takes to double your money.

Let's use our examples from above:

Stock or stock mutual fund returns an average of 10%

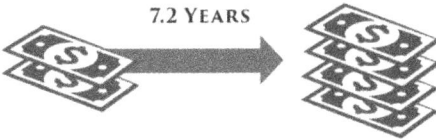

7.2 YEARS

IF A STOCK OR STOCK MUTUAL FUND RETURNS 10%,

THEN WE COULD EXPECT TO DOUBLE OUR MONEY IN 7.2 YEARS

72 DIVIDED BY A 1% MONEY MARKET RETURN EQUALS A 72-YEAR DOUBLE OF YOUR MONEY

A Bond Portfolio returns an average of 5%

14.4 YEARS

IF A BOND PORTFOLIO RETURNS 5%,

THEN WE COULD EXPECT TO DOUBLE OUR MONEY IN 14.4 YEARS

72 DIVIDED BY A 5% AVERAGE RETURN ON YOUR BOND PORTFOLIO EQUALS A 14.4-YEAR DOUBLE OF YOUR MONEY

A Money Market returns an average of 1%

72 YEARS

IF A MONEY MARKET RETURNS 1%,

THEN WE COULD EXPECT TO DOUBLE OUR MONEY IN 72 YEARS

72 DIVIDED BY A 10% AVERAGE RETURN ON YOUR STOCK OR STOCK MUTUAL FUNDS EQUALS A 7.2-YEAR DOUBLE OF YOUR MONEY

In other words, using our example, a dollar invested in stocks would be worth two dollars in 7.2 years. This becomes especially important when you factor inflation into the dialogue. Long-term inflation (or the rising cost of stuff) has historically been about 3%[4]. Although current inflation is very low, most financial professionals recommend factoring in a 3% inflation rate when planning for your retirement as a margin of safety for your future spending needs.

If the price of stuff increases by 3% per year, that means the price of stuff doubles about every 24 years. This makes sense if you simply look at the price increases in a US postage stamp. In 1990, a stamp cost a quarter. Twenty-five years later, the price had increased to 49 cents, nearly doubling in cost. What this means for us, the 401(k) savers of the world, is that for us to afford to buy the same stuff in retirement that we do today, our money needs to grow at a rate better than inflation. Since some expenses like college tuition, food, and health care are inflating at a rate much higher than 3%, it's critical for us to have a portion of our 401(k) exposed to higher-return potentials, like those that can come from owning stocks or stock mutual funds.

Let's apply the Rule of 72 to another example to help better visualize the magic of compound interest and the power of doubling.

Let's assume a nice conservative 7.2% return on stocks or stock mutual funds beginning at age forty with a $200,000 account value, and compare that to a 3.5% bond portfolio and a 0% cash portfolio. Our goal is to accumulate as much as possible and not start spending our money until age seventy.

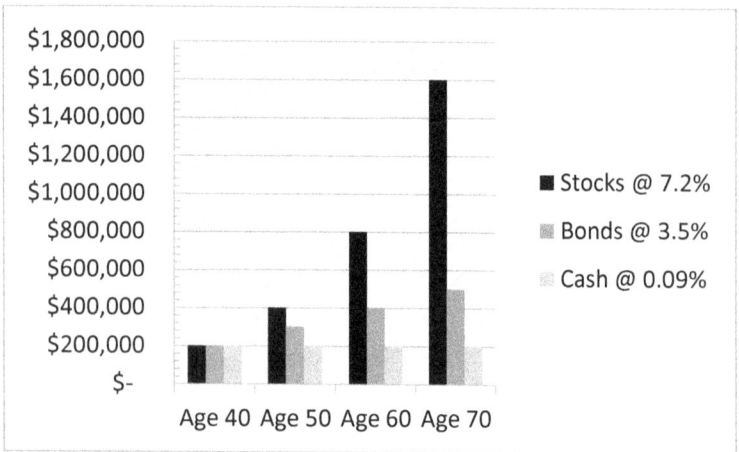

- Age 40 $200,000
- Age 50 $400,000 (double #1)
- Age 60 $800,000 (double #2)
- Age 70 $1,600,000 (double #3)

At seventy, as the proud owner of a $1.6 million retirement account, you may now feel more secure in your ability to replace your working income with retirement income from your 401(k). The best part of this example is that it does not take into account any additional contributions you might make along the way. Adding the maximum contribution to your 401(k) every year can make this doubling effect happen even faster.

The Rule of 72 is a helpful little math formula that should give you a bit more confidence and clarity in what lies ahead for retirement.

Happy doubling!

I pulled a pair of pants that I hadn't worn in a long time out of my closet. As I slipped them on, I reached into the pocket and to my surprise found a $20 bill. It felt like I had just won the lottery.

What a wonderful way to start a day. The rest of the morning was spent thinking about how I was going to treat myself with this little surplus. I decided I would use it to spoil my taste buds with a big fat greasy burger. The best burger I have ever wrapped my teeth around was just a few miles down the road at a little family-owned farm-to-table restaurant called Hawks. They serve their burger on a salty pretzel roll and top it with bacon, mushrooms and short ribs--what they like to call The Trifecta. The only thing missing is a sprinkling of crushed Lipitor mixed into the burger patty. Regardless of the three pounds I would gain from this one meal, I felt the need to indulge a little.

Wouldn't you?

Several of my hard-working friends have recently told me similar stories of finding a few extra bucks lying around--not the way I found my extra $20, but rather in their household budget.

Household finances for many people are still not nearly where they were prior to 2008, but many friends and neighbors I talk to seem to be finding a little more "room" in the family budget. Jobs are coming back, wages are finally increasing, gas prices are down, and the stock market keeps bumping up against all-time highs. Most "201(k)s" from 2008 are back to healthier pre-crisis 401(k) values. It's really uplifting to know many Americans are getting back on track, finding a bit of a surplus each month after the bills are paid.

If this is your situation, maybe you're asking yourself *what should I do with the extra cash?*

The first thing to consider is beefing up your savings account. I recommend an emergency reserve fund of at least six months of income. If there's one thing the first fifteen years of the 21st century have taught us, with the dot-com bubble bursting followed by the Great Recession of 2008-2009, it's the importance of having a financial safety net to fall back on.

If you have been able to refill your emergency fund to sufficient levels, where might you look next to use your surplus money? Here are some tips to consider.

Surplus money tip 1:
Invest in your most valuable asset: you

You are your most valuable asset. In our office, we advise our private clients to invest ten percent of their income every year in personal development. You must invest in yourself to maintain the best possible *you* there is.

There are a variety of ways we advise our clients to do this. For example, if you're physically healthy, you'll perform better at work and enjoy a happier overall lifestyle. Consider joining a local gym or hiring a personal trainer once a week, or working with a nutritionist to craft a healthier diet plan.

If you're mentally and emotionally clear on your unique abilities and the most effective way to apply them, you'll achieve peak performance in your personal and professional life. Consider hiring a life coach or a business coach if you lack this clarity in your talents.

Maybe it's time to consider taking a course at your local community college to enhance your industry knowledge, or possibly help you move in a completely new professional direction. Maybe you'd like to hire a good web designer and invest a few hundred bucks in a good domain name to launch your own web-based business. Perhaps it's time to tap the artist within you, embrace your creative qualities, and start writing a book, song, or screenplay.

Uncovering your unique abilities and applying them to building your own business could be the most profitable investment of all — not just in dollars and cents, but also in the satisfaction and confidence that comes with being your own boss and delivering real value to your community.

Another investment in yourself that requires no money whatsoever is reviewing the commitments or activities you're involved in to see how they still serve you. If certain commitments occupy your time and no longer move you toward your goals, consider eliminating them from your life. There is no greater investment in yourself than creating time to pursue passions that engage your unique talents.

Surplus money tip 2:
Increase your 401(k) contribution
(or start contributing if you're not already)

If you have a small surplus every month of, say, $125, you could consider increasing your 401(k) contributions by $200 per month. Since it takes about $200 of before-tax earnings to net $125, this extra amount will have a much smaller impact on your take-home pay than you might think. This pre-tax addition to your 401(k) could add as much as $140,000 to your balance over twenty years (assuming a 10% long-term rate of return). In addition, many employers offer a match of some kind; for example, they contribute 50 cents to your retirement account for every dollar you put in. More generous companies even match you dollar-for-dollar. An extra $200 could result in an additional $100 match by your company. That extra $300 per month could add as much as $205,000 to your 401(k) over the next twenty years. That's some real dough to rack up as a reward for your discipline.

As a reminder, the maximum you can currently contribute to a 401(k) plan is $18,000 if you're under age fifty. If you're not contributing the maximum amount every year, you have room to increase your contributions, and reap the rewards of a more secure financial future.

Surplus money tip 3:
Make a dent in debt

If you're carrying significant consumer debt, it makes sense to put a plan together to pay it off with your extra money. As much as we encourage people to maximize their 401(k) savings, if you have high-interest credit cards, it's smart to tackle these debts before increasing your 401(k) contributions.

Simply put, the stock market has a long-term average return of 10-11%. If you're paying interest to a bank or a credit card company that's higher than that, it makes a ton of mathematical sense to work toward eliminating the debts first. There's no sense earning 10% on your extra money, to only turn around and pay more than 10% interest on debt you hold.

Start by paying your smaller debts first to claim that first emotional victory. See how much you can pay off each month, while at the same time engaging the pain of discipline to keep from buying more stuff and negating the great work you're doing.

However, when it comes to longer-term debt (like a mortgage), given that we have historically low rates for loans of that mature, it would make more sense to put your extra money into your retirement savings, like your 401(k) or your IRA.

An extra $20 found in the couch cushions or laundry is a wonderful surprise. Enjoy a nice lunch, or treat yourself to something fun. But when it comes to finding a little surplus in your household budget, like more and more people are doing today, make disciplined choices that can have a longer-lasting effect on your financial well-being.

You'll be very glad you did!

A young family friend approached me about buying stocks. He wanted to invest $2,000 in a good stock or two as a way to start his life-long journey of saving and investing. But he really didn't know what a stock was or how to go about buying it.

For new investors, buying stock does not have to be a difficult proposition. You should understand four basic things to get started:

- What stock is

- How to purchase stock

- A few simple ways to identify good stocks to own

- The basic rules of stock investing

What is stock?

Plain and simple, *stock is a share in the ownership of a company*. Stock represents a claim on the company's *assets* and *earnings*. As you acquire more stock, your ownership stake and influence within the organization become greater. Whether you say *shares*, *equity*, or *stock*, it all means the same thing. If you buy a company's stock, it technically means you own a tiny sliver of every part of the enterprise, from the furniture, to the trademark, and every client contract.

As an owner, you are entitled to your share of the company's earnings as well as any voting rights attached to the stock. For every share you own, normally you are entitled to one vote when it comes to electing the board of directors. The board oversees hiring and firing the key leadership, who in turn run the day-to-day decision-making and operations of the company. This vote happens every year at the annual shareholders' meeting.

Shareholders who do not attend this meeting (which is usually most shareholders) receive a voting *proxy* in the mail to cast their ballots, similar to the absentee ballots used in government elections. The more shares you own, the more influence you have over who makes the day-to-day decisions within the organization. For example, if you own one share of stock, you will have very little say about who gets elected to the board. But if you own ten million shares, you may have substantial influence over who gets to run the company and how they choose to run it, especially if ten million shares represent a large percentage of the total number of shares issued by the company. Heck, you might even find yourself with a seat on the board of directors!

How do I purchase shares of stock?

Shares of stock are bought and sold every day across the world in marketplaces much like your grocery store. Instead of selling milk and bread, these markets, known as *exchanges*, buy and sell stock on behalf of investors. These exchanges are also referred to as the *secondary market*, because this is where existing (used) shares of stock are bought and sold.

Stock exchanges are run by specialists who know how to transact a purchase or a sale of stock shares between a buyer and a seller. These specialists earn a commission for helping someone buy or sell their shares on this exchange. Generally these specialists work on behalf of a brokerage firm; for example, Charles Schwab. If you are a client of Charles Schwab, you would instruct your broker to buy or sell shares of stock on your behalf. Your broker would submit an electronic order for this "buy or sell" transaction to his trading desk. The trading desk would then work with an exchange specialist to execute the trade with another investor.

Brand new shares of stock can also be purchased, but only when a company issues new shares of stock through a process called a *public offering*. Basically, a company hires a big investment bank to analyze their balance sheet and tell them how much their company is worth. Then the bank breaks that total net worth up into shares, and sells those shares to investors through an initial public offering (*IPO*).

The owners of privately-owned businesses will sometimes choose to convert their companies to publicly-owned businesses to raise large sums of money. This cash is most commonly used to expand their business, buy other businesses, or to simply cash out and retire. In effect, these business owners trade a large portion of their ownership and control of their company for cash that they can use immediately as they see fit.

How do I identify good stocks to buy?

First, be a loyal customer.

Start your search with a small list of publicly-owned companies whose products or services you use, and have been using for quite some time. Chances are you're not the only one who values what these companies do (or make).

What brand of coffee do you drink every day? What type of car do you drive? What type of smart phone or tablet do you own? These are very good places to start narrowing your list of choices.

Second, *identify great leadership.* Once you narrow your list down to a handful of companies you spend your money with, learn everything you can about the leadership of those companies. The growth of an organization starts and ends with great leadership. Does the team create a company culture that rallies around a common purpose? Do they consider their employees their greatest asset? Do they create opportunities for entry-level employees to become CEO of the company? Does the entire organization work together to create an amazing experience for their customers? Do the leaders and the employees of the company believe that they are in business to do more than just make money for themselves?

Finding answers to these questions can be done with some simple Google searches and a bit of online reading. Simply search on "corporate culture of XYZ Company" and see what pops up. Answering yes to all of these questions is the key to determining if the stock of a company is worth investing your hard-earned dollars.

Third, *seek dividends.* A *dividend* is a profit distribution made by a company to all of its owners or shareholders. Companies generally pay dividends to their owners when they are healthy, stable, and highly profitable over a substantial period of time, and they want to use this dividend to share the success of the company with all shareholders.

Dividends can be paid in two ways: cash or stock. *Cash dividends* are paid directly to shareholders and can either be taken as cash or reinvested to buy more shares. *Stock dividends* are paid out in the form of additional shares of stock, usually in fractional amounts.

Here are two examples.

Let's say you own a hundred shares of ABC Company. ABC Company has announced they are paying shareholders an annual dividend of $.85 per share. For your hundred shares, you will receive a check for $85 each year until the dividend amount changes. You can also choose to use your $85 to purchase more shares at whatever the current market price is for the stock. This is a simple example of a cash dividend.

Now let's take the same scenario with your ownership of ABC Company. You own a hundred shares and ABC Company's board of directors declares that they are issuing a dividend in the form of .3 shares per share owned. That means you will receive thirty additional shares of ABC stock.

Companies will sometimes make stock dividend distributions rather than cash dividends if much of their cash is tied up in business-expanding investments and not available for dividend payments. Either way, companies that pay regular, growing dividends in the form of cash or stock are a sign of a very healthy organization.

Basic rules for stock owners

Once you have found the right stock, you must follow the four rules of stock ownership.

1) **Never buy a stock that you would ever have a reason to sell**. What I mean by this is you must feel completely aligned with all aspects of the organization, from leadership to products to balance sheet. If a company makes a great product that is selling like wildfire, yet they have a heretic at the helm as CEO, at some point that lack of strong leadership will come back to hurt the company (possibly when the product falls out of favor).

2) **Be patient**. Stock prices do not necessarily grow in a straight line overnight. It's like planting a seed in a garden; it takes time and a whole lot of patience for that seed to become a delicious fruit ready for harvest.

3) **Buy a few more shares every month no matter what**. The key to long-term success with purchasing stock is to gradually accumulate shares over your entire career of investing. Several chapters ago, we discussed the benefits of systematic monthly investments with the same dollar amount, or what is commonly called *dollar-cost averaging*. By accumulating shares of a company over time, you reduce your risk and lower the average price you pay per share.

4) **Never mix your emotions with stock ownership**. This one is pretty self-explanatory. The decision to own a fraction of a company is a business decision. There is nothing more dangerous than allowing emotions to dictate a business decision.

If you really love a certain company because their product is an important part of your life, the leadership is doing the right thing, and they pay dividends to their owners, chances are you may have found a winner. Remember, as an owner of stock, you are making a commitment to own part of this company for a long time. Your shares will fluctuate in value, sometimes going up and down for no apparent reason whatsoever. Check your emotions at the door and be prepared to buy more. And if you can't leave your emotions out of the mix, consider hiring a financial advisor who specializes in purchasing individual stocks.

This advisor can also be especially helpful when it's time to consider selling your ownership in these companies. Like all business owners, there will come a time in your life when divesting yourself of your shares will be a necessary strategy to provide the kind of retirement you will likely want. Talk to your financial advisor about exactly how your exit strategy from corporate ownership should be structured.

Congratulations.

You are one step closer to becoming an owner in some of the most amazing companies in the world!

Many of my clients own bonds, and as the stock market becomes more and more volatile, more clients ask questions about owning bonds for a larger portion of their portfolio.

Interestingly enough, I have found that most people I meet know very little about bonds, and for the most part, what they know is not necessarily true.

A common belief people have when they think of bonds is that they're safer than stocks.

They can be. But they can also be riskier.

Let's go back to basics and dive under the hood of the bond as an investment. Bonds are quite different than stocks. Whereas a stock is a unit of ownership in a corporation, a bond is a form of debt. Typically bonds are issued by companies, cities, schools, and governments as loans, or IOUs. The difference is you, the investor, serve as the bank. You loan them your money and they promise to pay you back in full at a certain date in the future through regular interest payments.

A company may sell bonds to purchase new computers or build a new facility. A school may sell bonds to build a new gymnasium. A city may sell bonds to build a new park. A state may sell bonds to repair highways. The federal government issues bonds to finance its increasing debt load.

Bonds tend to attract more conservative investors because of the steady stream of interest income they earn, as well as stock investors who flock to the perceived safety of bonds when the stock market becomes too volatile. However, despite the regular income payments investors receive through bonds, bonds are not risk-free. Some bonds can even carry more substantial risk than stocks.

Risk in owning bonds is not very well understood by most investors. This risk comes in a few different varieties: credit risk, interest rate risk, call risk, reinvestment risk and inflation risk.

Credit risk

What is the likelihood the bond issuer will make good on its obligation to pay you back upon the stated maturity of the bond, as well as make interest payments each quarter or month?

Less credit-worthy issuers will pay a higher yield, or interest rate. That's why the riskiest issuers offer what's called high-yield, or "junk" bonds. They must pay you a higher interest rate to offset the higher risk that they may default on their loan to you. Those at the opposite end of the spectrum, with the best histories of repaying debts, are deemed investment-grade bonds, and generally pay a lower interest rate because you will likely not need to worry about a default.

The safest bonds from the standpoint of credit risk are those issued by the US government, known as Treasuries. These bonds are backed by the "full faith and credit" of the federal government, and are deemed virtually risk-free. The government has the ability to raise taxes and/or issue new debt to pay their existing debts, something most entities do not have the power to do. As such, a Treasury bond will pay a lower yield than a bond issued by a corporation or a school district.

Interest-rate risk

The longer the bond, the higher the interest rate you're paid. Bonds that mature in thirty years tend to pay more interest than bonds that mature in five years. You're being paid more for keeping your money tied up for a longer period of time. However, it's important to know that owning a longer bond (twenty or thirty years) exposes you to greater interest-rate risk.

Interest rates have the single largest impact on daily bond prices. As interest rates rise, bond prices fall. When rates climb, new bonds are issued at the higher rate, making existing bonds with lower rates less valuable in the current marketplace. The good news is that if you hold on to your bond until maturity, it doesn't matter how much the price fluctuates because the bond issuer agreed to pay you back the full face amount (amount you invested originally) of the bond when it matures. But if you need to sell your bond on the secondary market before it matures, you could get less than your original investment back if interest rates rise and your bond becomes less valuable. The farther away your bond is from maturing, the more sensitive its price will be if interest rates fluctuate.

Call risk

Some bonds have a built-in safety feature for bond issuers, referred to as "call protection," that gives them the ability to "call" their bond away from you and return your money. If interest rates drop, this call feature allows issuers to basically erase their current debt and reissue new bonds at a lower interest rate. It's like having the option to refinance your debt.

The reason this poses a risk to investors is that many bond holders base a substantial portion of their retirement income on the interest they receive from their bond holdings. If a retiree has a large bond position called away, and must now buy lower-paying bonds, it could have a drastic effect on the amount of income the retiree receives.

Reinvestment risk & inflation risk

Similar to call risk, reinvestment risk can hurt bond investors significantly if interest rates drop dramatically. Back in 1981, when then-Federal Reserve Chairman Paul Volcker was battling to contain hyperinflation, thirty-year bond yields topped 15%. Twenty-seven years later, during the crisis of 2008, the thirty-year yield plummeted to an all-time low of 2.55%.

Imagine if you had a million dollars invested in thirty-year bonds in 1981. You would have been earning nearly $150,000 each year in interest payments. Those bonds would have matured in 2011, and if you were to renew them, your interest payment would drop to $25,500. Not only would your income have dropped substantially, but so would the amount of purchasing power your million dollars had.

In 1981, a postage stamp cost eighteen cents. By 2011, a stamp cost increased by more than double to forty-four cents. Your million-dollar bond investment today is worth about half[4] of what it was worth in 1981, meaning it will buy you about half of what it could have bought you thirty years ago.

Now that we have reviewed the risks of owning bonds, let's briefly describe the different types of bonds you can invest in and some of the common terminology associated with bond ownership.

As discussed earlier, *Treasuries* are issued by the US government and are considered the safest bonds on the market. As such, you won't collect as much in interest as you might elsewhere, but you don't have to worry about defaults. They're also used as a benchmark to price all other bonds, such as those issued by companies and municipalities.

Treasuries are available in $1,000 increments and are initially sold via auction, where the price of the bond and how much interest it pays out is determined. You can bid directly through TreasuryDirect.gov [5] (with no fees) or through your bank or broker. They also trade like any regular security on the open market.

Treasury Bills, or T-bills, are a short-term investment sold in terms ranging from a few days to 26 weeks. They're sold at a discount to their face value ($1,000); however, when T-bills mature, you redeem the full face value. You pocket the difference between the amount you paid and the face value, which is the interest you earned.

Treasury Notes are issued in terms of two, five and ten years and in increments of $1,000. Mortgage rates are priced off of the ten-year note (more commonly called the ten-year bond even though it's technically a note).

Treasury Bonds are issued in terms of thirty years. They pay interest every six months until they mature.

Treasury Inflation-Protected Securities (TIPS) are used to protect your portfolio against inflation. TIPS usually pay a lower interest rate than other Treasuries, but their principal and interest payments, paid every six months, adjust with inflation as measured by the Consumer Price Index. It's best to hold these in a tax-deferred account such as an IRA because you'll have to pay federal taxes on the increase in your bond value, even though you don't get the principal back until maturity. When TIPS do mature, investors receive either the adjusted principal or the original principal, whichever is greater. TIPS are sold with five, ten, and twenty-year terms.

Savings Bonds are probably some of the most boring gifts out there, but it can't hurt to understand how they work. You can redeem your savings bonds after one year, and within up to thirty years. They're currently offered in two flavors, both issued by the US Treasury: EE savings bonds and I savings bonds.

EE Savings Bonds earn a fixed rate of interest (currently 3.4%) and can be redeemed after a year (though you lose three months interest if you hold them less than five years), but can be held for up to thirty years. When you redeem the bond, you'll collect the interest accrued plus the amount you paid for the bond. They can be purchased in the form of a paper certificate at a bank for half of their face value (for example, a $100 bond can be purchased for $50) in varying increments from $50 to $10,000. If they're purchased online, they're purchased at face value, but can be bought for any amount starting at $25.

I Savings Bonds are similar to EE savings bonds, except that they're indexed for inflation every six months. These are always sold at face value, regardless of whether you buy paper or electronic versions.

Agency bonds are not quite as safe as Treasuries, yet they are often safer than the most pristine corporate bonds. They're issued by government-sponsored enterprises, like Fannie Mae and Freddie Mac (mortgage-backed bonds) and Sally Mae (student loan-backed bonds). Because these companies are chartered and regulated in part by the government, the bonds they issue are perceived to be safer than corporate bonds. They are not, however, backed by the "full faith and credit" of the US government like Treasuries, which would make them virtually risk-free.

Municipal bonds, or munis, are issued by states, cities and local governments to fund various projects. Municipals aren't subject to federal taxes, and if you live where the bonds are issued, they may also be exempt from state taxes. Some municipal bonds are more credit-worthy than others, though some munis are insured. In this case, if the issuer defaults, the insurance company will have to cover the tab.

Corporate bonds are bonds issued by companies. Corporate debt can range from extremely safe to super risky.

Coupon is another word for the interest rate paid by a bond. For instance, a $1,000 bond with a six-percent coupon will pay $60 a year. The word coupon is used because historically some bonds actually had a paper coupon attached to them that could be redeemed for the payment, especially prior to 1990.

Par is also known as the face value of a bond; this is the amount a bondholder receives when the bond matures. If interest rates rise higher than the existing bond's rate, the bond will trade at a discount, or below par; if rates fall below the bond's rate, it will trade at a premium, or above par.

Duration is a measure of a bond price's sensitivity to a change in interest rates, measured in years. Bonds with longer durations are more sensitive to interest rate changes. If you're in a bond with a duration of ten years and rates rise one percent, the price of your bond will decline by ten percent.

This is one of the greatest unknowns to investors who think bond buying is super safe. It is in this type of low-interest-rate environment that bond investors can really be caught off guard. If rates begin to rise and bond investors are forced to sell their bonds prior to maturity, they can be handed significant losses due to the rising rate environment. This can be even worse for those bond investors who own their bonds inside bond mutual funds. When owning bond mutual funds, you no longer have the option of holding your bonds to maturity. A high-duration bond mutual fund could experience complete free-fall in a sharply rising interest rate environment.

Maturity is the date your bond matures and you receive all of your principal back. Some bonds may get called away before their maturity date; but either way, you receive your par value back.

Like all possible investment tools, bonds may have a place inside a portfolio to provide everything from current income to appreciation potential. However, use caution when purchasing bonds. And if you're a novice investor, I recommend you not go at it alone. Bond yields have been falling for nearly thirty years, which means prices have been rising. Many experts believe the bond market will be the next bubble to pop when rates begin to rise. And given that the bond market is considerably larger than the stock market, a bond bubble pop would be catastrophic.

If you need some guidance purchasing bonds, I recommend working with a financial advisor in your community. Here are some resources to help you find an advisor with knowledge of investing in bonds:

- Certified Financial Planner Board of Standards [7]
- WiserAdvisor.com [8]
- The Financial Industry Regulatory Advisory's Broker Check [9]

Exchange Traded Funds (ETFs) are a big topic at my firm. Clients and friends ask us quite often to help them better understand what these really are. I am amazed at how many people ask the question, because so many of them already own ETFs inside their 401(k)s, whether they realize it or not.

ETFs have been around since the early 1990s, but really did not become popular in 401(k) plans until about ten years ago. Although ETFs have begun to gain popularity, the ETF market still pales in comparison[10] to the mutual fund market: about $1.9 trillion in ETFs versus over $15 trillion in mutual funds.

To truly understand ETFs, let's take a look at their history and see the product evolution that led to their creation. ETFs were born from the progression of actively-managed mutual funds and passively-managed index funds. Let's look at both of these product types first, so that we may better understand the distinctions between ETFs.

Actively-managed mutual funds

A mutual fund is a big basket of individual investments like stocks (such as IBM, Proctor & Gamble, Apple, Coca-Cola, etc.). Every day, the fund issues new shares to those who want to own a "slice." It is the simplest way for investors to diversify their money with a small investment amount: most fund companies let you purchase shares for as little as $2,000.

The best way to understand this structure and its benefits is to think of an extra-large pizza pie with a handful of toppings:

pepperoni, sausage, olives, mushrooms, onions, and peppers (sort of makes you hungry, right?). You cut the pizza into eight slices and share it with a few friends. Each slice has a sampling of all the selected toppings on it. The best part of having multiple toppings is that if one is bad--say, the olives--people can just pick them off without ruining the whole slice.

Mutual funds work much the same way. If all your retirement money was invested in one individual stock, and that stock became worthless, you would be in big trouble. But if your retirement money was invested inside of a mutual fund, where you had a "slice" that contained samplings, or fractional shares of hundreds of stocks, you would be much less concerned if one went bad.

So who manages mutual funds, and what are they trying to accomplish?

Mutual funds rely on a portfolio manager, or a team of portfolio managers, to actively manage investments on behalf of others--usually for a hefty fee. According to Morningstar, the average annual fee charged for a mutual fund is 0.9%[11]. This is also called an expense ratio. In addition to the expense ratio, a mutual fund can cost an additional 1.44% per year in transaction fees[12], which are the costs portfolio managers incur for buying and selling stocks inside their funds. These costs can be more difficult to determine on a fund-by-fund basis because fund companies are not required to publish these additional expenses in their fund prospectus[13].

In exchange for paying upwards of 2.5% to 3% per year in total fees, portfolio managers hope that their active management can take advantage of mispriced stocks or trends in the market to beat the overall market return. Unfortunately for most portfolio managers and their fund investors, history has proven that hope is not a successful strategy, as the majority of fund managers have failed to outperform their benchmarks.

Passively-managed index mutual funds

Imagine the pizza we used to describe an actively-managed mutual fund. Now, instead of a handful of toppings on it, imagine every topping ever created: five hundred, to be exact. Each slice would have a small sampling of five hundred different toppings. I know what you're thinking: it would almost be impossible to distinguish the taste of one topping from another. But that was the strategy of John Bogle, founder of Vanguard Funds, who launched the first index mutual fund in 1976.

Mr. Bogle believed that it was nearly impossible for any manager to beat the markets by actively trading a handful of stocks. He also believed it was in an investor's best interest to stay fully invested in the entire market at all times, riding it up and down for a long period.

Bogle's first index fund tracked the Standard and Poor's 500 Index (S&P 500). The fund was called the Vanguard 500. By owning all five hundred stocks of the S&P 500, Bogle was able to promise investors that his fund would keep up with the broad index of stocks. Since his fund was not actively managed, it cost very little to operate, which translated to a very low cost for investors.

Wall Street and the financial advisory community were not fans of Mr. Bogle and his new invention. They quickly slandered the Vanguard 500 Fund by referring to it as "Bogle's Folly." It was the belief of Wall Street and most financial advisors that their primary job was to beat the broad market and that Bogle's invention was a joke. Ultimately, the joke was on Wall Street and the financial advisors[14]. Few actually were able to beat their benchmarks and Bogle's Vanguard 500 Fund, especially once they added in their 2.5%-3% each year in fees.

Index funds have gained in popularity over the past three decades. Today there are hundreds of index funds, each tracking their own benchmark and typically at a tiny fraction of the cost of actively-managed mutual funds. They are some of the most popular fund offerings inside company-sponsored 401(k) plans.

What is an ETF?

An ETF is a type of index fund. It has the same goal as an index fund: to provide investors with a low-cost product that offers broad market returns. There are two important differences, however.

First, index funds are like traditional mutual funds in that they are only priced once per day, at the close of the market session. The average price of all the underlying securities is calculated after the market closes, and the fund company posts the net asset value per share (NAV) based on the aggregate of all those prices. In contrast, ETFs are a fixed basket of securities that trade all day on the stock market, with the basket itself behaving more like an individual stock. The price of that basket of stocks can fluctuate all day based on the underlying values of the holdings within the ETF. This can give investors much greater liquidity, which gives them the ability to buy or sell shares quickly and at any time the market is open, rather than relying on a mutual fund or index fund that only prices itself once per day after the market closes.

The second main difference is the cost of trading mutual funds and index funds compared to the cost of trading an ETF. Mutual funds and index funds often have significant transaction fees associated with buying or selling shares. Although most ETFs also incur transaction fees, some trade commission-free.

ETFs Version 2.0

As ETFs have grown in popularity, they are increasingly designed to do more than just mimic an index fund. Sector-specific ETFs, where all the holdings are from one specific sector (like healthcare or technology), have become quite popular. Many fee-only financial advisors have adopted ETFs into their practices as efficient tools to actively manage client portfolios and gain exposure to multiple sectors of the market.

But "do-it-yourselfers," beware. There are risks and complexities associated with buying and selling ETFs. If you are a DIY investor and you want to have the flexibility of an ETF's low trading cost, and performance similar to an index fund, it's best to use only the largest, most widely-traded ETFs--the ones designed to match well-known benchmarks. The smaller sector-based ETFs often have much less liquidity on a daily basis, as fewer shares are traded compared to the big index-based ETFs. Also, like mutual funds, ETF performance can vary widely from issuer to issuer--even those that seem to track the same benchmark or sector.

ETFs have become the next great innovation in the mutual fund/index fund universe. They can be very efficient investment products, and are showing their rise in popularity by popping up more and more inside company-sponsored 401(k) plans.

If you own a 401(k) and you choose to go at it alone selecting your ETFs, please do your homework. Managing an active portfolio of ETFs is not for novice investors with a weekend hobby. Work with a professional whenever possible.

One of the most viciously targeted and often scrutinized financial tools in existence is the deferred annuity. Various factions on Wall Street, in the media, and even in government and politics have made it their mission to discredit the deferred annuity as a viable investment option for a portion of one's retirement savings. They often cite high fees, illiquidity and product complexity as the primary reasons why the wretched deferred annuity is the average investor's arch-nemesis.

I have a problem with this generalization of an investment tool.

Is a hammer good or bad? I hope your answer is, "Depends on how it's used." If I use a hammer to rebuild a deck in your back yard, it's a good tool. If you stiff me on payment, and I use that hammer to destroy your new deck, the hammer is a bad tool.

The same can be said about deferred annuities. The deferred annuity is simply a tool--a rather complex one, but nonetheless, a tool. The key to making it work right is to apply it correctly to the right circumstance. Unfortunately there are too many financial advisors out there who do not fully understand the best applications for deferred annuities, and they often sell them to clients when they are not appropriate vehicles. But how can you blame the deferred annuity, or deferred annuity provider in this case? It's not the hammer's fault if I hit you over the head with it. It's my fault.

So quit picking on the annuity, please, and let's place blame where it needs to be placed: on selfish financial advisors whose only concern is making a healthy commission for themselves.

Let's take a step back and look at what an annuity actually is and where it may be appropriate for a portion of your retirement savings.

We'll start with a simple definition of the word *annuity*. An annuity is synonymous with income. Typically an annuity is a form of income that is created by transferring an asset into an income stream. Think of it like a trade. An investor trades a certain asset--say, a $250,000 IRA-- to an insurance company, which, in return for that asset, delivers the investor an income stream, usually promised for life or a fixed number of years (10, 20, or 30).

There are two main categories of annuities: immediate and deferred. Extrapolating our original definition of an annuity as income, one can easily conclude what the primary difference is between immediate and deferred annuities: an immediate annuity is one that begins payments *now*. A deferred annuity begins payments *later*. That's pretty simple, right?

Let's take it a step further.

Within the immediate and deferred annuity camps, there are two sub-categories that define the type of interest (or income) you receive in exchange for your asset: fixed and variable. The difference between fixed and variable (as one might guess) is that fixed annuities pay a set, locked-in income amount for the duration of the annuity contract, and a variable annuity pays an income that can change throughout the duration of the contract.

Now that we've covered the basic terms, let's put a few of them together to show you how different annuities are designed.

Fixed lifetime immediate annuity: Income now that a pays a fixed interest rate for life.

Deferred variable annuity: This is an annuity that creates income later in life by allowing you to defer that income at a variable rate, or a changing rate of return. Often that variable rate of return is delivered in the form of variable sub-accounts, which are mutual fund-like investment options inside deferred variable annuities that you and your advisor choose with the hopes for a good return over time, and which ultimately provide you with income down the road.

Fixed indexed deferred annuity: This is a much more complex structure that combines some features of a variable annuity with a fixed annuity to defer income for the future. It provides a fixed minimum return (assuming you buy the rider that provides this benefit), but also allows you to capture a portion of a stock or bond market index return to boost that future income amount.

There are many more types of annuity products on the market today. When used properly for the right reasons, annuities can be one of the best investments you ever make, especially if your goal is to create guaranteed income to last your entire lifetime.

Let's face it: retirement is completely on our shoulders. That means it's up to us to figure out how to replace our career income with retirement income, once we get to the point in life where *have-to's* get replaced by *want-to's*. Foundational expenses in retirement like housing, food and medical care must be covered by foundational income sources (pensions if you're one of the lucky ones, Social Security, bond interest, rental income, etc.). Should you find a gap between your estimated foundational expenses and foundational sources of income, an annuity can be an excellent tool to fill that gap. Discretionary expenses like travel, dining out, second homes, etc. can be based on the remainder of your retirement assets to create the discretionary income you need; those assets are typically exposed to more risk-based assets like stocks, bonds, mutual funds, ETFs and real estate.

Annuities can be very complex tools, and they certainly require the assistance of a professional. This person must have much more than just excellent product knowledge. He or she must also intimately know the details of your life, so together you can determine if an annuity makes sense for you…and if so, what type. Trust is the key element, as you, the investor, must trust this professional enough to open up and be completely transparent about your aspirations, your lifestyle, and how you see your vision of your ideal future. Anything less than that can cause a bad fit between an annuity product and an investor, leading to a less-than-desired outcome.

Remember, a hammer is a great tool when used to build a deck, but it quickly becomes evil if it's used to destroy your deck against your wishes. Having a properly structured and funded annuity can mean the difference between a happy retirement traveling the world, versus a stressful retirement filled with uncertainty and undesirable part-time jobs.

Deep down, many of us like the peace of mind that comes with owning a pension. But few of us have corporate pensions. So we can look to annuities as the do-it-yourself pension option if that peace of mind is truly important.

> **RETIREMENT: (N) *RE-TIRE-MINT*:**
> **AS DEFINED BY OUR FIRM AND OUR CLIENTS: A MAJOR LIFE**
> **TRANSITION POINT WHERE ONE HAS ACHIEVED FINANCIAL**
> **INDEPENDENCE AND A CLEAR VISION OF PURPOSE.**
> **OCCUPATION BECOMES *CHOICE RATHER* THAN NECESSITY.**

Planning for retirement is much more than saving money. It is a preparation process that requires time, dedication, discipline and contemplation.

A few generations ago, retirement planning seemed simpler. One worked for thirty years, usually for the same organization, and by age 65, reached the ceremonial finish line. Life expectancies once in retirement were about 7-10 years. A secure retirement was promised and provided through pensions, health care and Social Security. Time was often spent in year-round sunshine playing tennis, golf, or bridge, and then meeting friends at Tony Roma's for the Early Bird dinner at 4:30 pm. This period of life--what has been referred to as the "Golden Years"-- was golden because of its simplicity and comfort. Retirement was defined by an age and a promise.

Today, just a few generations later, the landscape of retirement has completely changed. Some might argue it has changed for the worse; some think it has changed for the better. With life expectancies reaching into the mid-to-late 80s, it's becoming common to see a retirement last twenty or more years. As more people even reach their 90s and 100s, retirement can last as long as forty years. For many, that equates to more time spent in retirement than time invested in the working years preparing for retirement.

For those who plan properly, the 20-40 years "after work" can have substantial meaning and purpose. It can allow one to feel incredibly fulfilled by having a massive impact on family and future generations, even more so than the time spent "working" the previous thirty years.

The path to proper retirement planning requires preparation in three areas:

- Financial preparedness
- Choice and control
- Purpose

Financial preparedness

Paying for life in retirement is almost completely on our shoulders now. Pension benefits have virtually vanished in the private sector, and they have been significantly reduced in the public sector. Our Social Security and Medicare programs are running on fumes and their future is bleak[15]. Both were social welfare programs created after the Great Depression of the 1930s to keep the elderly (with very short life expectancies) out of poverty. At the time, life expectancies were around 60 years old[16], and there were nearly 160 people working to support every one person receiving benefits.

Now life expectancies are much longer, and because of the roughly 77 million baby boomers reaching retirement, the ratio of worker to retiree has been dramatically reduced[17] to approximately 3:1. Over the next decade or two, this ratio could be reduced to one worker for every one retiree. This will require radical changes in both Social Security and Medicare, if not the complete elimination of one or both as they exist today as a retirement benefit for everyone. Many politicians and business leaders support the idea of means-testing to qualify for benefits, in effect reverting back to the original reasons why these programs were created: to keep retirees out of poverty.

Financial independence now requires a lifetime of financial preparation. For today's 65 year-old to live comfortably on $100,000 per year for the rest of his or her life (assuming they no longer want to work), one would need approximately $2.5 million saved to minimize the risk of running out of money, if we exclude Social Security. For today's 40-year-old planning to retire in 25 years, that same $100,000 lifestyle today will need to be $200,000 in 25 years just to buy the same stuff (thank you, inflation). That will require retirement savings of $5 million. This is certainly attainable, but it requires the discipline of long-term saving and avoiding the indulgences of overspending on meaningless stuff.

Choice and Control

Retirement can be a choice and it can happen on your terms, doing it when you want to, how you want to, and where you want to. Retirement is also something that needs to be completely redefined based on your own personal meaning.

Years ago, retirement meant "nothingness;" a few rounds of golf, a gold watch, and then you were gone. Today, retirement could be the most significant period in one's life, especially if it happens on purpose. Planning for choice and control becomes a reality when we can define *why* we want to retire.

Steve Jobs is a great example of someone who retired at a very young age. Everything he did, especially in the latter half of his life, was about choice. Steve didn't have to work. He was financially prepared for retirement by his late 30s. Despite having enough money to sit on a beach sipping margaritas for the rest of his life, Steve Jobs chose to transform the way the world communicates. The effect of his purpose--his *why*--has been felt all across human civilization. Not only did he turn Apple into the most valuable company in the world, he made face-to-face conversation a reality for nearly all of Earth's modernized population.

My parents, Henry and Jill Grishman, are also retired. Like Steve Jobs, they have chosen and maintained control over their retirement. My mother, Jill, was a school teacher who retired in

2010 to care for her parents and spend more time with her grandchildren. My father, Henry, has been retired for nearly fifteen years (based on my definition of retirement), yet at age seventy he still goes to his office almost every day at the Jericho Union Free School District in central Nassau County, New York.

Henry has been a school superintendent since 1977, and is currently one of longest-serving superintendents in the country. He is the best at his craft and he loves his job each and every day. Henry is very clear on his why, and as a result, he has had a direct impact on shaping the lives of thousands of children over a four-decade career. My parents have been such incredible role models for me in defining retirement and doing the necessary things to be in a position of choice and control by age 55.

Not bad for a couple of school teachers! It is their example that I use most to guide clients in defining their why, and preserving as much choice and control over their own retirement.

Despite Steve Jobs' and my parents' ability to choose and control their retirement, there are certainly factors outside of one's control that can force someone to consider retirement before they are ready. However, long-term preparation and attentiveness to one's true unique abilities can minimize the burden these unforeseen circumstances can place on a forced decision to retire. This is the most critical planning piece that should be well-defined if having control and choice are to become a reality. The key element to this planning is attaching financial preparedness to finding purpose.

Purpose

Many retirees, as well as people in their 30s, 40s and 50s working toward retirement, struggle most with the emotional and social changes that come with the transition into retirement. Retirement is no longer about "nothingness." It's a stage of life that can often last longer than one's working years. Therefore, investing the proper time to reflect on "what's next" is a critical part of the retirement planning process.

Is "next" a second career? Is it writing a book, volunteering, or going back to school? Is it traveling the world, or learning how to fly a plane, or building furniture? The key to answering this big question is to sit quietly and listen carefully to what your soul tells you. It's not a thinking process; it's a feeling process.

In our wealth management practice, we help clients begin the inner dialogue about what's next by helping them define their *true wealth*. We do this by taking families through a proprietary system called the GGI Wealth FORMation Process^{SM}. Our process allows clients to measure their true wealth in four major categories: Family, Occupation, Recreation and Money. The Family category is about defining the most important people in one's life and becoming acutely aware of the impact they have on one's happiness. We'll come back to Occupation, as that is the key part of the purpose work that needs to happen prior to retirement. Recreation is the category that defines the fun in life: what one enjoys doing most with the people one cares about most. Money is the category where we identify and document one's belief system about money--how money serves the most important aspirations one has in life. We also establish the steps necessary to accumulate and protect the amount of money identified to support one's true wealth.

Occupation is the category of true wealth that is often simpler to define in the working years of life. Occupation is about how people outwardly share their unique abilities for the benefit of their family, their community, and the entire world. Occupation is expressed in a variety of ways: working, volunteering, and coaching youth sports, to name a few examples. Occupation is a key ingredient in one's overall happiness and fulfillment in life. As one approaches retirement, Occupation can become more difficult to define. People are often challenged to figure out what's next as they transition from "have to" mode to "want to" mode.

Do you know what your new occupation will be in retirement?

Purpose work becomes an important component to the retirement planning process, as it ties the three parts of planning into one holistic definition of retirement. This can often take years of hard work and self-examination. With proper planning and coaching, one's true purpose will show up and all of the pieces of retirement will fall into place.

When people are clear on who they are, what they're supposed to do, and most critically, *why* they're supposed to do it, choice, control, financial preparation, and purpose all come together to create a dynamic plan that leads to a retirement of happiness, gratification, and significance.

This is no small task. The biggest mistake made in the retirement planning years is developing a belief that retirement planning is simply about saving money. That could not be farther from the truth. Putting all three pieces in place happens at different points in life, with some definite overlap.

Creating the Thirty-Year Plan for a Retirement on Purpose looks like this:

AGE 30

FINANCIAL
PREPAREDNESS

AGE 40

CHOICE
& CONTROL

AGE 50

PURPOSE

AGE 60

AGE 65

Financial planning and preparation generally begin around thirty years old. If done correctly and consistently, this should take approximately 25 years to complete. Purpose work usually begins around forty. For some clients, finding a well-defined purpose for retirement can happen quickly, sometimes as soon as five years or less. For most, purpose work is a 10-20 year process of clearly defining one's unique abilities and exploring how those abilities can be applied to 80% or more of the time spent in Occupation. Once people have established financial preparedness and are clear on their purpose, choice and control over *why* retirement, *when* retirement, *how* retirement, *who* retirement, and *what* retirement all become crystal clear.

There is great satisfaction in this moment of retirement "on purpose". For many, it is the greatest victory in life. It is most common to experience it somewhere between 55-65 years old; however, it can happen sooner. It happened for me at 38.

This moment can create a feeling of satisfaction and self-fulfillment that extends way beyond any previous accomplishment, including marriage and raising kids. This definition of retirement is available to anyone who chooses consciously to build a Thirty-Year Plan.

Retirement is no longer provided to us. We must choose to create our Golden Years. It takes planning, dedication, discipline, persistence, and time. It also takes a real pro by your side to guide you, a wealth coach to help you stay accountable to enjoying the journey and achieving the ultimate success in life: a retirement on purpose.

Guiding others on this journey has become my occupation. And I do it on purpose.

There are many definitions of retirement circulating through dictionaries across the globe that you can easily find with the click of a mouse. Wikipedia[18] defines retirement as "the point where a person stops employment completely. A person may also semi-retire by reducing work hours." Merriam-Webster[19] defines it as "the act of ending your working or professional career; the act of retiring; the state of being retired; the period after you have permanently stopped your job or profession."

You read my definition of retirement in the last chapter, which is "a major life transition point where one has achieved financial independence and a clear vision of purpose. Occupation becomes choice rather than necessity."

Is retirement a homogeneous period of time in one's life that is simply defined by not working anymore? If that's the case, then planning should be pretty simple, right? All we need to do is calculate how much money we need to save to provide for life after work and all will be okay, right?

Wrong!

In fact, the definitions I found online could not be farther from the truth of what retirement really is. Society as a whole has failed both the baby boomers and Generation X by selling retirement (and the process of planning for it) as a simple money issue--accumulating money and distributing money, or a fancy way of saying *saving and spending*. Financial advice has been driven by a belief that basic asset allocation (another fancy term that means spreading your money out over several kinds of investments) with your retirement savings will accumulate over time (saving) and provide you with modest distributions (spending) that should last your entire life. Television commercials depict this dream on a daily basis: retired couples strolling on the beach, or playing golf, or traveling with friends, followed by a celebrity voice describing promises of investment and insurance strategies to help you pay for these golden moments of recreation.

But defining and planning your retirement is so much more than how to pay for your travel.

Over the past twenty years, I've seen people of all ages struggle with the emotional side of retirement as well as the transition through the different tiers of retirement. With a little discipline and a winning strategy[20], the savings side of retirement planning is pretty simple. On the other hand, there are some not-so-simple parts to the retirement puzzle the financial planning industry is failing to help people with:

- Figuring out what you're going to do for the rest of your life

- The right timing of your retirement

- Managing the different phases of a multi-decade retirement

As I discussed in the previous chapter, people are living longer. Retirement is often a 20, 30, or even 40-year proposition. It is now possible to experience a retirement that lasts longer than the pre-retirement years of working and saving for it. Planning for retirement requires a much deeper strategy besides a good target series fund in your 401(k), followed by a rollover to an IRA and a four-percent withdrawal rate.

We teach our clients that retirement is comprised of three distinct phases that all have a different effect on your savings and your emotional well-being. We call them:

- The Go-Go Phase
- The Slow-Go Phase
- The No-Go Phase

Each phase requires proper planning as our lifestyles change dramatically from one phase to the next. There's no set formula that dictates how long each phase lasts, and the transitions between them are sometimes not very well defined. Proper planning is paramount so that when a transition does occur, you are ready and prepared. I realize that the following explanations of these three phases are somewhat simplistic and rather broad. Each person we meet experiences some commonality with all other retirees, but also has unique needs and transition timelines from one phase to the next. These portrayals of the three phases of retirement are based on twenty years of observations from my partner and me in our private practice and within our own families.

The Go-Go Phase

The Go-Go Phase is the time often defined by freedom, constant activity and recreation. Traveling to see the grandkids, visiting the bucket list destinations, and dining out with friends are all signature experiences of the Go-Go Phase of retirement. Work can still be a big part of the Go-Go Phase, but now all work happens out of choice rather than obligation. Assuming people have uncovered their true unique abilities and found a way to give them to the world, they can spend a significant portion of their lives in this "doing" space.

Although living expenses can be high in the Go-Go Phase, typically these costs do not come with significant inflation. Travel, food, and entertainment have not seen a great deal of inflation the past few decades, so planning for this phase is quite different than the latter phases of retirement, where inflation is moving at hyper-speed. Allocating a portion of your retirement savings to the Go-Go Phase can be set at a more conservative pace, where growth keeps up with or slightly exceeds core inflation (1-2%). Generally we see our clients incur an asset burn rate (withdrawals from retirement savings) close to or even slightly greater than their living expenses prior to retirement.

One of the key components to a solid multi-phase retirement plan is to set aside a full year's worth of cash to finance an entire year of living expenses. The common practice implemented by your average run-of-the-mill brokerage firm is to take monthly distributions from your retirement savings to cover your expenses. It is my belief, based on working with Go-Go retirees, that this is a flawed strategy; it puts too much pressure on retirement savings to perform beyond the desired withdrawal rate each and every year.

Let's look at this a bit closer.

The average withdrawal rate recommended by Wall Street brokers and mutual fund companies is generally 3-4% annually[21] (broken into monthly or quarterly distributions). They claim that if you maintain these modest withdrawal rates, you have a low probability of outliving your assets. But that doesn't tell the whole story. During the decade of 2000-2010, the first official decade of massive baby boomer retirements, the market barely squeaked out a four-percent annual average return. Add to that paltry return the annual expenses of the mutual funds your broker would have you in, and you were likely barely in the positive.

In the past two years, I have met many retirees who came to me after retiring in the mid-2000s with less than half of what they started with at retirement. Why? Too much stress on their portfolio in a decade of horrendous returns to produce current income through monthly withdrawals. It's simply more proof of yet one more completely flawed belief that benefits the brokerage firms and mutual fund companies more than the retirees they're supposed to be serving.

As fiduciaries devoted to serving the best interest of our clients, we implement a strategy that sets aside an entire year's worth of cash at the beginning of every calendar year, allowing a client (especially those newly retired and in the Go-Go Phase) to access what they need to live on and allow the remainder of their portfolio to work without the stress of producing current income.

The Slow-Go Phase

We have observed that most of our clients enter the second phase of retirement somewhere between 5-15 years after retirement officially begins. Physically they are still in good shape. They have reached a point in life where they have "been there, done that" and enjoy staying closer to home. They invite the children to come visit. They cook more than they dine out, and they really get connected to their home and a small community of inner circle relationships. Couples will often remodel their home to reflect how they want to use it at this point in their lives. Cost of living tends to decline a bit, as they do not spend as much on travel and leisure. However, a home renovation in the Slow-Go Phase could weigh heavily on one's assets, so careful planning is necessary.

Planning for the Slow-Go Phase requires a look into the things in life one truly enjoys…the simple things. Long walks, Sunday drives, watching the grandchildren play Little League baseball, a favorite movie, cooking a favorite dish. The Slow-Go Phase also comes with great contemplation. It is a time in one's life where people decide if they have truly lived their life's purpose. They sit back and enjoy seeing their legacy in their children and grandchildren. Financially they can take their foot off the gas pedal as their spending generally slows. This phase can have the least demand on assets, so setting aside a portion that modestly grows beyond inflation is wise.

When planning for this phase, we set aside a portion of client assets that we intend to invest for a little longer period of time. Clients generally do not need access to this money for 5-15 years. Therefore, we tend to focus on tax-efficient growth strategies to maximize the growth potential so that these assets can do their job and pay for those living expenses incurred throughout the Slow-Go Phase.

The last phase in retirement is one that can last ten or more years. One of the realities of life is that at some point, our bodies will age and not function as they used to. We may spend most of our time at home and/or visiting doctors. We will need more medical care and possibly help around the house with everyday tasks like cooking, cleaning, bathing, and driving.

This can also become the most expensive phase of retirement. Financial preparation for this phase requires some complex planning separate from the planning required for the first two phases. Your savings must grow at a much greater rate than core inflation, as prices of health care and homecare are accelerating at a rate much higher than core inflation. Despite inflation decreasing in health care since the enactment of the Affordable Care Act[22], health care costs still grow at a rate that is almost three times that of core inflation[23].

Once the financial preparation is complete, the more difficult task of preparing for the emotional transition between the Slow-Go Phase and No-Go Phase must begin. This is no easy conversation, but it's certainly one that can help minimize the fear of unknowns surrounding old age and dying.

It is critical to understand that retirement is not a standardized time in life that simply means life after work, funded by monthly withdrawals from retirement savings accounts with a splash of Social Security on top. It's potentially a multi-decade, multi-phase time in life that requires customized planning; planning that encompasses both financial and emotional preparedness. An oversimplified, one-size-fits-all investing blueprint built by large mutual fund companies, banks and brokerage firms is simply not good enough. You worked too hard for too long to accept that kind of mediocre approach to planning your Golden Years.

Defining retirement and properly planning for it is not a small task. It might feel so overwhelming that you decide to let it sit on the back burner to deal with later. Unfortunately, later often becomes too late, and something happens where people are forced to make decisions they are not prepared for.

So let's get retirement off the back burner and take a small step together. Forget Wikipedia and Webster. Let's define *your* retirement. I'll even give you a head start by letting you see my personal definition of retirement one more time:

Retirement: (n) re-tire-mint: a major life transition point where one has achieved financial independence and a clear vision of their life's true purpose. Occupation becomes choice rather than necessity.

The next step is up to you. Choose wisely how to approach planning, and make sure your financial advisor understands you are a person with complex needs--not just a financial statement that produces monthly retirement income. For help finding the right financial advisor, check the list of resources at the end of Chapter 15.

Have you been recently widowed? Are you in the midst of a difficult divorce? Are you a stay-at-home mom ready to re-enter the workforce? Are you a business owner about to take your company public? Have you recently experienced the death of a parent? Are you a recently married and considering the start of your family?

If you are a woman and answered yes to any of these questions, you are experiencing a major life transition. It is important to realize that as a woman facing a new life challenge, you now have very special financial needs. And you are certainly not alone.

Divorce is the most common transition that brings a woman to our doorsteps for financial advice. This makes complete sense as the divorce rate in the state of California is now a staggering 75%[24]. That means three out of four marriages in California end in divorce.

Widowhood is the next most common life change we see when we meet a new female client experiencing a major transition. The average American woman lives almost five years[25] longer than the average American man. The Women's Institute for a Secure Retirement[26] also reports that half of all widows become so by age 65, and that they are more likely than men to suffer a drop in income after the death of their spouse.

Living through a major life transition creates very strong emotions. Whether these emotions are positive or negative, there is nothing more dangerous to one's financial well-being than combining major money decisions with emotions. You will likely need triage strategies for handling necessary financial decisions during your major transition.

Although your circumstances are unique to you, women in transition face similar challenges.

Most women I meet going through major life changes tell me that feel like they are in limbo; like they are stuck in a thick fog and can't see or think clearly. If you feel this way, you are not alone. Most people get stuck in limbo as a basic coping function to protect themselves from stress and negative emotions.

But this state of numbness can also be dangerous when the fog gives us permission to make bad choices with our money, or avoid handling the important stuff like paying bills. Whether bills go unpaid, or you start spending impulsively, you can find yourself looking back with an incredible amount of regret. We've met women who have completely depleted their IRAs to travel the world with their best girlfriend to help cope with the loss of their husbands. We have also met women who have not paid their utility bills or mortgages for months and found themselves facing serious credit consequences. Meanwhile, women in transition may also be in a vortex of swirling, conflicting advice from well-meaning friends and family.

Over the many years our firm has helped women in such situations, we have found five basic tips that can help nearly all of them.

Tip #1:
Give yourself time

Don't sell your home. Don't re-allocate all of your retirement savings. Don't invest your life insurance benefits. Give yourself at least six months to upwards of a year to work through your "fog" before you make any substantial financial decisions. Remember, there is nothing more dangerous to your financial well-being than making big money decisions while emotions are running high. You should seek professional advice on what decisions you can defer and what decisions you cannot defer. When in doubt, take your time.

For help finding professional advice, start by asking a close friend, family member or trusted advisor (e.g. CPA or attorney). If you have no one to rely on for advice, consider visiting www.cfp.net to find a Certified Financial Planner (CFP®) in your neighborhood who specializes in helping women in transition.

Tip #2:
Ask for help

Although I recommend you delay large financial decisions, there are everyday decisions that have to be made whether you feel up to it or not. Paying your bills is the biggest. If you are struggling to keep up with your daily financial responsibilities, ask for help. Consider asking a close friend or family member to step in and take over this function for you for a while. Or if you are not comfortable with that, consider hiring a bookkeeper or accountant to handle it for you. Of course this might incur some cost, but it will be well worth it if it means protecting your credit and keeping you current with your monthly financial obligations.

Tip #3:
Buy yourself financial safety

Keep your money as liquid as possible, especially if you are experiencing a transition as a result of death of a spouse, a divorce, or a significant windfall (sale of a business, loss of a parent, etc.). Liquid assets, such as cash and short-term investments, give you the safety net you need in an emotional time of transition. After six months or a year, your needs will change. You will want to preserve as many options as possible, and staying liquid and "safe" does just that. However your money was invested in the past may or may not suit your needs now.

Tip #4:
Try to stay healthy

You will make better choices if you eat right, sleep enough, rest or meditate, and make time for exercise every day. The only person you need to focus on at this point is you. Whether you have children or others that depend on your care, you can only be your best for them if you take care of you first and foremost.

Tip #5:
Protect yourself

Unfortunately, there are devious people in our world who look for an opportunity to take advantage of people in transition, especially women. Many of the women I work with have unintentionally vented their emotional vulnerability during their life change, often through outlets like social media. Be very careful of the people offering help. Always have a trusted friend, family member, or advisor as a sounding board before you choose to engage anyone or any business to help you.

Often, devious financial advisors will try to approach a woman in transition to take advantage of her new potential financial windfall. Before you engage a financial advisor that approaches you, visit The Financial Industry Regulatory Agency to perform a background check on him or her[27].

Hopefully your transition is the result of something great happening in your life, like having your first baby or selling your business. Unfortunately, the women we are introduced to are often experiencing a very painful event. Regardless of whether your big life transition is positive or negative, the tips listed above are the five most important things to consider when it comes to your financial well-being.

I wish you peace and prosperity, and I know with confidence that one day your fog will lift, and you will have the courage to take that necessary step forward in the next great stage of your life.

Some mistakes are more costly than others.

I once made a mistake by not listening to my mom. She told me to put on an extra sweater because it was going to be cold that day. Sure enough, she was right. I suffered miserably for an entire day. I froze my tail off in school because I chose to ignore her.

This is definitely a mistake most kids make and learn from. I thought I had learned from it by wearing the extra sweater the next day. But many years later, I made a similar mistake that nearly cost me my life, as well as the lives of my wife and my best friend.

It was a superbly warm day in July of 1996, with a gentle breeze and not a cloud in the sky. A large group of my family and friends were hiking a section of the famous Appalachian Trail in the White Mountains of New Hampshire. We were on our way to the 6200-foot summit of Mt. Washington, the tallest peak in the Northeast.

The majority of our group chose the easy route; I wanted to tackle the Webster Cliff Trail, known for its torturous switchbacks and demanding rock wall ascents.

My wife and best friend decided to join me. Since the three of us were choosing a more difficult climb, we lightened up on gear, despite being warned that bad weather could blow in at any time. The trek was scheduled to take eight hours, after which we would meet up with the rest of the group at the Mizpah Springs

Hut, near the base of our final ascent to the summit of Mt. Washington.

About four hours into our hike, I regretted not listening to the warnings and not learning the lesson my Mom had tried to teach me fifteen years earlier. In an instant, we were caught in a freezing rain storm with nothing more than our tee shirts to keep us warm. The temperature plummeted almost fifty degrees as the once-gentle breeze turned to gale-force winds, and icy rain began pelting our bodies from all directions.

We hunkered down in some brush to try to keep dry and warm, hoping the storm would blow over soon. After hours of holding one another and shivering, the storm finally subsided and we resumed our trek to Mizpah Springs.

Nighttime had descended on us. We were cold, tired, hungry and without a flashlight. With two miles in front of us and the early stages of hypothermia setting in, we knew our mistake could cost us a lot more than being cold in school for a day.

Our lives were at stake.

We began to panic. After four grueling hours of faltering around in the dark, we made it to Mizpah Springs. It was almost midnight--ten hours after we were supposed to arrive. We were drenched and trembling, and very lucky to be alive.

My wife didn't speak to me for the rest of the trip.

With the silent treatment and a good scare being the worst consequence I suffered, one might say I got off lucky. But the realization swept over me that this mistake almost cost me the two people I cared most about, as well as my own life. I vowed never to make that mistake again.

Now, many years later, I take my sons hiking every summer in the Northern California Redwoods. We always over-pack food and clothing just in case the worst might happen again. Luckily, it hasn't.

Most people I know can relate to this experience--making the same mistake twice in life, where the consequences the first time around were virtually meaningless, yet the second time around was a whole different ballgame.

Do we really learn from our mistakes? Or does actually choosing differently depend upon the "cost?"

Take the Great Recession of 2008 as another example.

Did we really learn from the mistakes that created that crisis? Or was the cost not nearly great enough to prevent it from ever happening again?

As painful as it was for millions of families, I do not believe the recession was costly enough for society as a whole. Markets have recovered. Jobs have reappeared. Home prices and 401(k) values have returned to hit new highs. And many people have forgotten what it feels like to lose money in the stock market.

On one hand, part of American society has learned from this experience. Consumers are not spending nearly as freely as they were prior to the recession, despite gains in some sectors. People who bought homes they could not afford, maxed out their credit cards to furnish them, drove expensive cars and toys, and then lost it all, have certainly shown signs of learning their lesson by making smarter choices today. But what about Wall Street brokerage firms and the oligarchy in power? Have they learned anything? Were their mistakes costly enough to change?

The economist, author, and blogger Tyler Cowen has written that we might need to get used to the idea that our economy will continue to struggle as a result of not fully learning our lesson. In a May, 2015 *New York Times* blog post[28], Cowen wrote

"...there is a much more disturbing possibility that could turn out to be more accurate: namely, that the recession was a learning experience that we haven't fully absorbed. From this perspective, the radical and sudden changes of the financial crisis were early indicators of deep fragility and dysfunctionality. Slowly but surely, we may be responding to these difficult revelations by scaling back our ambitions for the economy — reinforcing negative trends that were already underway. In this troubling view, we have finally begun to discover some unpleasant truths. Borrowing a phrase from the University of Toronto economist Richard Florida, it's possible that we are experiencing a Great Reset."

A "Great Reset," as Cowen describes, is basically a period in which workers, employers, and policymakers slowly modify what they can expect from the economic engine. This concept or current environment has also been called the "new normal" by well-known bond fund manager, Bill Gross.

The questions I will continue to ask 401(k) savers to ponder are these:

- Did 2008 cost enough?

- Will we, as a society, emerge from this Great Reset with the true intention to avoid the gluttonous mistakes we all made that led to the financial chaos that brought this great country to its knees?

- Or was it not costly enough, and might we be on the brink of repeating the same mistakes again?

- If that's the case, how do you protect your 401(k) from becoming a 201(k) again[29]?

When I read about firms packaging and selling sub-prime auto loans to yield-starved investors[30], I become skeptical that things will truly change. But when I read consumer confidence is low[31] and retail sales are weak[32] because more people are saving their money rather than spending it[33], I get a bit more hopeful.

Maybe, just maybe, we will emerge from this Great Reset with a new economic value for saving and being stewards of our wealth, rather than continuing the spendthrift behavior and excessive borrowing that seem to have driven our economic growth historically.

Today, 81 million Americans participate in some sort of retirement plan at work, putting part of their paycheck away for a time when they'll need it to replace their working income. These plans are commonly referred to as 401(k), 403(b) or 457 plans. For the sake of this discussion, we'll simply refer to all of them as 401(k).

There are several common mistakes people are making with their 401(k) that are easily avoidable. Bypassing these pitfalls can mean the difference between having a secure retirement and being forced to have a late-life career as a greeter at a big box retailer.

Mistake #1:
Cashing out your 401(k)

One of the worst things you can do with your 401(k) account is to cash it out.

With so many people changing jobs every few years, the temptation to cash out a small 401(k) balance is very high. Data from Fidelity Investments, the largest 401(k) provider out there, shows that 35% of their plans' participants cashed out their accounts in 2014 when leaving their jobs[34].

Holy cow! That's frightening!

A 401(k) is supposed to be a retirement savings account, something to be there for you when you no longer work to produce income. It's not meant to be another savings account to accumulate money temporarily. That's what banks are for! With fewer Americans receiving the gift of guaranteed pension income in retirement, and the average Social Security benefit figuring about $1,340 per month as of November 2015[35] (that's only about $15,900 annually), most of us need to be saving up lots of money on our own for retirement.

Fidelity also shared that among its plan participants in their 20s, 30s and 40s, the average cashed-out account balance was $14,300. What would have happened if those dollars remained invested?

Imagine a 35-year-old worker who just changed jobs and was planning on retirement at age 65, giving herself thirty more years to save. If that $14,300 was rolled into an IRA or her new company's 401(k) plan, and left alone for thirty more years, and it grew at the rate of about ten percent (the long-term historical average of the stock market), it would grow to nearly $250,000 by the time she reached age 65! And that's without putting another dime into it. If $5,000 were contributed each year along the way, the end result could be greater than $1.1 million.

Cashing out a 401(k) account worth $14,300 to satisfy some short-term need is the most expensive way to get your hands on money. Not only will a saver be faced with horrendous tax bills, but she will rob herself of somewhere between a ¼ million and a million dollars for her retirement.

Ouch!

Mistake #2:
Getting advice from the wrong source

Nothing is more crucial to the success of one's 401(k) than by getting the advice of a trusted professional.

But therein lies the problem. The employer who sponsors the 401(k) legally can't give you advice, and neither can the 401(k) plan provider. The problem here is that neither the employer who sponsors the plan nor the fund company that manages the plan wants to take on the liability of offering advice. If they were to do so, they would be required by law to take a fiduciary oath (putting your best interest ahead of their own) to you, the plan participant.

Despite sounding like a reasonable thing to do, most employers and fund companies refuse to take this fiduciary role of providing advice to plan participants. What winds up happening is retirement savers receive free "education" and then are forced to rely on their own skills as expert investors to make the decisions about what to invest in and when to make changes to their plan.

Who really has time for that?

Quite often retirement savers do not know where to turn. Most end up seeking financial advice from friends and family members. But even the most well-intentioned and insightful advice from these sources does not replace that of an investing expert, accountant or other retirement finance authority to aid with critical decision-making that will impact the entirety of a retiree's life.

Mistake #3:
Underestimating inflation

Do you remember how much a postage stamp cost in 1990? A quarter. Today a stamp costs 49 cents. That's almost a 100% increase in the last twenty-five years.

If your 401(k) nest egg is not earning enough to stay ahead of inflation and taxes, your retirement lifestyle is likely to get scrambled well ahead of its time. For your money to buy you the same amount of stamps today as it could have in 1990, your money would have to be growing at better than 3% per year. With most Treasury bonds and CDs paying well below that today, it's critical to explore equities and equity funds to stay ahead of long-term inflation so your money can buy you what you need in retirement. The scary part is that things like food, healthcare and prescription drugs are increasing in cost at a much greater inflation rate than postage stamps.

Mistake #4:
Operating on autopilot

As important as it is to invest a portion of your retirement savings in equities to maintain your purchasing power in retirement, you have to know what you're doing to be successful. This isn't for amateurs, as owning equities can be risky business.

Retirement savers often fail to properly adjust the investment vehicles in their portfolio as market conditions change. As a result, many of the big 401(k) providers have offered a solution to the old static approach of "buy and hold" called *target series funds*. These funds are designed to automatically adjust your portfolio each year as you get closer to retirement. In theory, this is a good idea. But who in their right mind would ever board an airplane that can only operate and adjust course with its autopilot feature? We still want a captain in the cockpit, right?

The same can be said about your retirement savings. It's a huge mistake to leave your retirement savings on autopilot in a target series fund. Here's why. As you move closer to your retirement date, target series funds automatically shift your money from stocks to bonds, giving you the perception that your money is being moved into safer asset classes. Nothing could be further from the truth. Bond prices are at all-time highs, and the majority of thinkers on Wall Street today believe the bond market is a huge bubble waiting to pop if interest rates move higher. Imagine having all of your assets slowly shifted to bonds and then two years before you're ready to retire, POP! The bond market implodes and you're left with half of what you were expecting to retire on. This is the risk you assume when you leave your retirement savings on autopilot in a target series fund.

In spite of this risk, nearly eighty cents on every dollar contributed to 401(k) plans gets allocated to a target series fund. It's easy to do, kind of like taking a multivitamin. Quite often people we meet will opt for something easier over something that requires a little more effort. I get it completely. Who has time to put more effort into investing? Yet most people I personally interview acknowledge the need to be doing more with their 401(k) savings. They just do not know how, and often lack the time to find a better way.

By the way, one of the largest and most widely selected target series fund, the Fidelity 2020 Fund, was down over thirty percent in 2008. That means if you had $1,000,000 in your 401(k) allocated to that fund, by 2009 it would have been worth less than $700,000.

Mistake #5:
Missing out on free money

One of the biggest 401(k) blunders is not taking full advantage of money that your employer is willing to contribute to your account. Many employers match any contributions you make on your own behalf up to a certain amount (usually 4-6%). This is free money from your employer, and it's worth the minimal effort to claim it.

Some employers also make profit-sharing contributions on an employee's behalf based on a percentage of your salary. Most of the time, you don't need to do anything to receive profit-sharing contributions. But with employer matching, it's critical to save at least enough to maximize the amount of your employer's contribution. Typical 401(k) plans will include provisions that match half of your contributions up to a maximum of six percent of your total salary, but some are much more generous, matching your contributions dollar-for-dollar or providing matching on even higher percentages of your total pay.

By not contributing at least the minimum amount to get the company match, you're leaving free retirement savings dollars on the table. Even a small employer match of $500 a year can add an additional $100,000 to your savings balance over thirty years.

Mistake # 6:
No Plan, Stan

Retirement savers often lack a financial plan that includes estate planning, budgeting, saving for their kids' college, life insurance planning, and lifetime income planning. It's challenging enough to allocate time to properly structuring your 401(k), let alone finding time to do all of the rest. But without this kind of comprehensive planning, there's very little chance for success in your retirement planning. There are so many financial matters that can arise over one's lifetime that can completely devastate a 401(k): unexpected death or disability, a hefty college bill, a new roof on a house, sudden layoffs, an unexpected child or grandchild. With proper financial planning, one can be prepared for all of these possibilities.

Few people I know have the courage to book a three-week family vacation with no plans but airline tickets. Most people also book hotel and dinner reservations, schedule activities, and arrange for transportation. Of course, every planned vacation encounters some bumps or changes to the schedule, but for the most part, we put many hours into carefully planning our vacations. Why wouldn't we? Vacations can be sizable investments in life-long memories. I simply recommend we put the same effort into planning our entire future, not just the fun parts like vacations.

There has historically been a lack of proper beneficiary and estate planning in the US, and it has cost Americans billions of dollars. According to the National Association of Unclaimed Property Administrators, state treasurers currently hold $32.9 billion in unclaimed bank accounts and other assets. According to the US Department of Labor, $850 million in 401(k) assets go unclaimed each year.

It is critical that 401(k) savers plan properly, starting with reviewing beneficiary designations on their plan often, so that their assets wind up going where they want in the case of unexpected or early death.

An old friend and I were having lunch. He seemed very frustrated when we sat down at our table. Before we even opened our menus, I asked him if there was something on his mind.

Without hesitation, he began sharing how his financial advisor had failed to keep up with the market, with the result that his retirement savings was significantly underperforming.

He was adamant about firing his advisor and hiring my firm to take over the day-to-day management of his portfolio.

After asking a few more questions and listening carefully, I was able to help my friend see that his portfolio was doing exactly what it needed to be doing for his retirement. I politely declined his offer. I knew my friend's advisor. This individual cares deeply for her clients, provides excellent service, and is extremely good at what she does.

My friend had unfortunately bought into one of three common myths that can really hurt retirement savers: *believing that you have to beat the market*.

More about that in a minute.

Even with good guidance from a professional wealth advisor, navigating Wall Street and the retirement savings sphere can be terrifying, unclear, and awash in myths for the average investor. With a 24-hour news cycle on television and instantaneous access to current market events on their smartphones, everyday retirement savers are often lured into believing what the media machine wants them to believe. I saw this firsthand having lunch with my old friend, and I see it every day in my conversations with others. Becoming aware of these mythological beliefs is a crucial first step for retirement savers to successfully traverse their way to a secure retirement.

Myth #1:
You must beat the market

One of the first discussions I have with prospective clients is a deep dive into the most important long-term goals they have for themselves and their families. Over the past twenty years of having these discussions, I have yet to hear someone tell me that their top goal is to beat the market or a market index.

People describe their vision of their ideal future, and seek help reaching certain financial thresholds that allow them to do the things they enjoy most with the people they love most. These important goals have nothing to do with beating an index. A good wealth advisor will help you establish a plan to reach these thresholds so that you can have what matters most in life. Reaching these goals is rarely, if ever, dependent upon beating a market index.

It's easy to understand where the myth that you must beat the market came from. As pensions started disappearing "en masse" in the 1980s and 1990s, more and more people began investing through vehicles like 401(k) plans and IRA accounts. This huge influx of new investment capital drove markets to all-time heights. In the 1990s, investors saw returns that often doubled their money every two or three years. As a result, more people flocked to the market as the 1990s came to a close, with hopes of creating enormous wealth. This led many to the belief that the success of their portfolio depended on *beating the market.*

The S&P 500 index has a long-term average of 10.2% per year. Wall Street brokerage firm mythology has many believing that this represents the entire market--that it's the bull's eye. According to the mythology, it's the primary responsibility of the advisor or portfolio manager to outperform this index each and every year as a result of what happened in the 1990s.

The reality is that the S&P 500 only represents a fraction of the broad market, made up of the largest five hundred companies in America. That's a very small slice of the overall broad market worldwide, and it's a return that requires taking on substantial risk with one's retirement savings to beat.

The whole concept of understanding risk relative to market returns is very misunderstood. Many people we meet are willing to take more risk in good markets and less risk in bad markets…except it doesn't really work that way!

I believe your long-term wealth is something you will acquire through *your occupation and your discipline to save money.* Your investment portfolio is a place for you to protect that wealth and make sure it maintains its purchasing power (beats inflation) over time. With long-term inflation at 2-3%, most retirement savers have the ability to reach their most important goals with far less return (and far less risk) than that of the S&P 500.

Your portfolio is likely the largest part of your savings, and should not be thrown completely to the stock market rollercoaster. It should be viewed as an investment vehicle designed to create *security, stability and predictability for your most important life objectives*. Trying to beat the market requires a gambler's mentality which could be extremely dangerous for one's financial well-being. Having a small portion of your overall portfolio allocated to "play money" or gambling money that takes substantial risks is fine. However, I recommend that this never be more than five percent of your total portfolio. In fact, you're better off taking that money to Las Vegas, rather than gambling with it in high risk stuff in the market. At least in Vegas you can gamble and be entertained at the same time!

Myth #2:
"Buy and hold" investing is the best approach

One of the most common myths propagated by Wall Street brokerage firms and mainstream media is the belief that you can simply put your portfolio on autopilot, staying passively invested while you ride the market waves up and down hoping it works out for you one day when you need it. The sales pitch supporting the myth of passive investing is very convincing: missing out on the 10-20 best days of the market each year can cost most of your return.

But the devil is in the details. What would happen if you also missed the 10-20 worst- performing days of the market each year? Your return actually increases! The buy-and-hold sales pitch leaves that part out. It also leaves out the reality that passive investing has failed millions of retirement savers twice already in the 21st century: once during the dot-com bubble of

2000-2002, and again during the Great Recession of 2008-2009. In both of those bear markets, passive buy-and-hold investors lost anywhere between 25-60% of their retirement savings.

Imagine seeing your million-dollar 401(k) lose $250,000-$600,000 right before you needed it to replace your working income.

Proper portfolio management requires a dynamic approach that matches the busy, dynamic lives real people live. As goals and market environments change, so must one's portfolio. A portfolio requires ongoing maintenance, monitoring and reallocating as trends in markets shift over one's lifetime. Betting solely on a passive allocation, "setting it and forgetting it," is a disaster waiting to happen come the next bear market.

Remember, Wall Street brokers and the big fund companies only earn their fees if you remain fully invested, passively riding the market waves up and down. The minute you adjust your portfolio to reflect a more defensive position (moving money to cash), brokers and the big fund companies lose. And they don't like to lose.

Myth #3:
Your broker has your back

A dear friend of mine lost her husband several years back. She told me how the best man in her wedding stepped in to help her right after her husband died. He was a lifelong trusted friend, and also called himself a "financial advisor." He assured her that he would put her money in something very safe, something that would be guaranteed not to lose money (his words, not mine).

At the time, that sounded good to my friend. But two years later when she needed $28,000 to replace the roof on her house, she found that she would be assessed a large surrender penalty for taking money out of that "safe" product her friend had sold her.

The product was an equity-indexed annuity. There is absolutely nothing wrong with an equity-indexed annuity if it's used in the right circumstances. But in my friend's case, she already had plenty of income from her rental properties, and her liquid assets were already tax-deferred because they were held in an IRA. There was no benefit to her to owning this annuity product whatsoever.

Then we figured out how much commission the advisor made by selling her this product: $40,000! He earned an 8% up-front commission by selling my dear friend an investment that was not in her best interest. And she hasn't heard from him since.

There are plenty of honest, ethical advisors in financial services. But there are also many who are not. Even within the sphere of "honest and ethical," there exists a fine line that can create a lot of conflict of interest when advising clients on what to do with their money. Simply put, any advisor who earns a commission that is paid by a mutual fund company, a brokerage firm, or an insurance company is opening the door for conflict of interest. And often it is the financial interest of the advisor that (legally) wins out.

Commission-based advisors are brokers. They are salespeople. They are licensed by the Financial Industry Regulatory Authority (FINRA) to sell securities for a commission, and are required by law to apply the "suitability standard" to a securities sale. That means that they must make sure an investment is suitable based on the client's age, investment experience, risk tolerance, and a handful of other factors before they can sell it to a client and earn a commission. But if that investment also happens to be the most expensive in its category because it pays a higher commission to the broker than some lower-cost equivalents, that broker can legally make that sale, even though it's not in the best interest of his client.

I rarely earn commissions for selling investment products. Only when it is in my clients' best interest and there is no other option, do we provide them with products that pay commissions from an insurance company. In some circumstances, we do not have a choice; for example, certain types of annuities that provide lifetime income can be in the best interest of some clients for a portion of their retirement savings. Often we meet people who are significantly under-insured when it comes to life insurance. Therefore we will generally recommend the least-expensive term policy we can find to fill their insurance gap. These products do pay us a modest commission. However, in situations like these, we uphold our obligation to serve the best interest of our clients and find the best products in the annuity and insurance world with no bias to any one insurer, regardless of the compensation to our firm.

With rare exceptions, the majority of our revenue comes from advisory fees we charge our clients directly. In most cases the only one paying us is our client. We are completely investment-agnostic, and generally recommend low-cost, index-based ETFs to our clients. It is our belief that investments are commodities, and the expenses associated with owning these commodities should be kept as low as possible. By charging fees directly to our clients, we are also obligated by federal law to uphold the fiduciary standard, meaning we must put our clients' best interest ahead of our own and eliminate all conflict of interest. By taking a fiduciary role in the lives of our clients, they know we have their backs.

Bottom line: the only way you can assure yourself that your advisor has your best interest in mind is to pick one that is primarily fee-based when it comes to the investable assets you entrust them to manage. If they use some commission-based products to run their business, that's fine, as long as they don't rely *exclusively* on these to earn their living. Salespeople who are 100% commission-based are fine for purchasing cars or furniture, but not for aligning with you on achieving your most important financial goals.

Finding a trusted advisor is an important rest stop on the road to building true wealth. Whether you are just graduating school and wondering how to buy a few stocks, or you're a seasoned investor ready to transition from building your wealth to protecting it, there are great advisors out there for you. Most people I meet have an incredible sense about others. Trust yourself; you'll know when you've found someone you can rely on to have your back with your wealth.

One of my early mentors used to have a funny spin on an old saying you might be familiar with:

"If it's too good to be true, it may not be. But if it's too good to be true, it's *definitely* too good to be free!"

PART IV:

CHALLENGING THE STATUS QUO:

A New Approach to Protecting and Growing Money that is Completely Counter to the Culture

For decades, the big Wall Street brokerage firms have promoted investment strategies based on hunches and intuitions. Their predictive-based strategies eventually evolved to using more academic-based theories (statistics and formulas) to try to predict better what "ought to" happen in the markets and how investors "ought to" behave as a result. Not only were these predictive-based and theory-based approaches to investing subjective, they were often very inconsistent.

I believe this approach is unsound and outdated, no longer serving the complex needs of investors in the 21st century. In Part IV, you will be introduced to a modern approach to saving, investing, and protecting your assets that goes one step further from the basics outlined in Parts II and III.

To illustrate, let's look at a story from Major League Baseball.

When Paul DiPodesta walked into the office of Oakland A's general manager Billy Beane, the game of baseball changed forever. It was 1999, and the A's were a small-budget team suffering a drought of post-season appearances. The collaboration of DiPodesta and Beane produced a transformation in how teams would manage for success moving forward. Their baby was a new statistical approach to player trend analysis called Sabermetrics--a transition in baseball history that was perfectly reflected in Michael Lewis' book *Moneyball*.

Prior to the pairing of these two very young, unlikely characters, front offices across the Major Leagues were filled with old, stodgy game veterans. General managers were usually former players who had been around the game for decades, sitting in their plush offices, smoking cigars, trying to figure out how they could keep their franchise superstars happy and productive. They made staffing decisions based on hunches and intuition, and money was king. The GMs with the biggest payrolls saw the most playoff opportunities for their teams. They rode their franchise players up and down the waves of a normal baseball career through streaks and slumps, hoping that streaks would last forever and slumps would end quickly. Players didn't move around very much. They stayed with one or two teams for the majority of their career, and retired with the hopes of managing in the dugout or the front office one day.

Before 1999, GMs used *some* statistics to support their hunches and intuitive tendencies. But these numbers were very subjective and often flawed, in the eyes of Beane and DiPodesta. Statistics such as stolen bases, runs batted in, and batting average, typically used to gauge players, produced an outdated view of the game relative to the statistics available at that time. Billy Beane and Paul DiPodesta began taking advantage of more analytical gauges of player performance to field a team that could better compete against the biggest payrolls in Major League Baseball.

Beane and DiPodesta began studying modern statistical analysis and player trends at great lengths. Their research found that on-base percentage and slugging percentage were better indicators of a team's ability to score runs and obtain offensive success. Beane was also convinced that these attributes were cheaper to secure on the open market than more historically valued measures such as power, speed and contact. His convictions caused great controversy between Beane and his scouts, who favored sticking with more traditional baseball wisdom of hunches and intuition. But Beane was hell-bent on flying in the face of the old ways; he was obsessed with going counter to the culture.

Despite a few years of constant battling, Beane eventually gained the support of his players, team owner and staff. By challenging the status quo of old-world baseball beliefs and radically changing the strategies that produce wins on the field, the 2002 Athletics and Billy Beane, with a $44 million payroll, were able to compete with the $125 million payroll of the mighty New York Yankees[36]. This new approach we've come to know as "moneyball" brought the A's to the playoffs in 2002 and 2003. They have remained one of the most consistently competitive teams in baseball ever since.

By the beginning of 2004, teams across the sport were adjusting their approach to selecting their rosters, mirroring the trend started by Billy Beane and Paul DiPodesta in 1999. Sabermetrics had taken hold of baseball and transformed the game as we know it today.

Thanks to new technologies and modern thinking that challenged the status quo, the front office leaders of baseball went from riding franchise players up and down the cycles of streaks and slumps, hoping for a shot at the playoffs, to applying trend analysis and statistical evaluation for determining their best chances at victory.

I use this story to illustrate some very direct parallels that we, as investors and retirement savers, need to consider. As I mentioned earlier, Wall Street brokerage firms have traditionally pushed investment strategies based on hunches and intuition—just like old-time baseball managers—and I believe they're off-base. The proof of their flaws came to light in the first ten years of the 21st century. These predictive and theory-based investment strategies created what's been called "the lost decade" for everyday investors and retirement savers. In fact, millions of people lost twenty, thirty, even forty percent of their life savings in 2008 and 2009 by quietly following the obsolete advice of big Wall Street brokerage firms.

Like Sabermetrics in baseball, there is a fact-based approach to analyzing trends and statistics in global markets that is available to investors like you and me. It will require you to begin questioning if there may, in fact, be a better way to manage your investments than what you currently are doing. Is there a strategy different from simply riding the market waves up and down, *hoping* for a shot at the playoffs?

In case you were wondering, there is.

Here's a little cap to the Billy Beane story. In 2003, John Henry, owner of the Boston Red Sox, became such a believer in Sabermetrics that he offered Billy Beane the largest paycheck ever for a baseball GM. Beane graciously turned it down so he could stay in Oakland. Of course, the Boston Red Sox went on to win the World Series the following season. By applying this new approach to trend analysis, Mr. Henry and his Red Sox were able to defeat the curse that had haunted them for decades.

Why was Mr. Henry such a believer? He recognized Sabermetrics as a trend-based approach similar to what he relied on for building and protecting his billion-dollar fortune in the commodities market. That strategy was called *mechanical trend following,* and it proved so successful that Mr. Henry used it to establish John W. Henry & Company, Inc. in 1981. His firm's approach to managing commodities for retail clients was based on automated trading decisions that were in response to trend reversals in each market's direction. Mr. Henry's primary goal was to *eliminate human emotion*, as well as subjective evaluation of such things as the so-called economic fundamentals that traditionally had been relied on by most commodities traders.

Henry's approach was almost identical to the one my firm subscribes to, with the primary difference being that we apply trend analysis to the stock market rather than the commodities market. We call it *fact-based investing,* and it applies quantitative trend analysis as the engine driving investment decisions. Fact-based investing is completely counter to the culture of Wall Street brokerage firms. Like Sabermetrics in baseball, it will ultimately transform the way people view and invest their hard-earned assets in the world of the stock market.

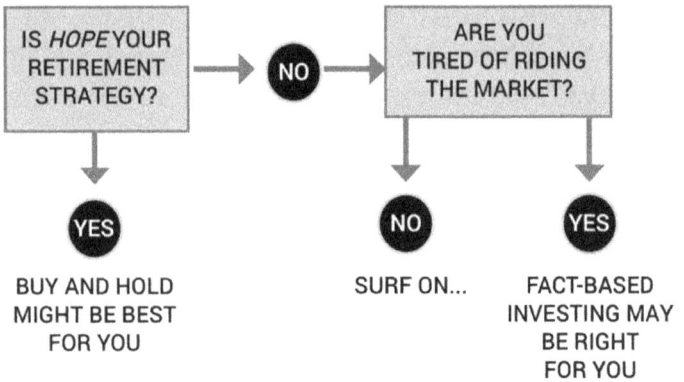

IS *HOPE* YOUR RETIREMENT STRATEGY? → NO → ARE YOU TIRED OF RIDING THE MARKET?

YES

BUY AND HOLD
MIGHT BE BEST
FOR YOU

NO

SURF ON...

YES

FACT-BASED
INVESTING MAY
BE RIGHT
FOR YOU

A good friend of mine recently asked for my advice about what to do with his life savings. It had become substantial and he was worried about losing it. He said, "Matthew, I understand that your life's work is about challenging the status quo; that you've developed a unique belief system about managing money and defining true wealth. Being able to quickly transition from offense to defense with my money seems smart, but everyone has always told me that buy-and-hold investing is the way to go. It's all I know, and it's what I'm comfortable with. Maybe you really can't teach old dogs new tricks."

You can't teach an old dog new tricks is one of the oldest idioms in the English language. I would bet big money that over my twenty-year career in financial services, I heard that saying at least a thousand times.

Well, I don't buy it. For one thing, old dogs can absolutely learn "new tricks." Life is constantly evolving and technology is improving exponentially, from communications to online banking and strategies for managing your 401(k).

When my son Miles was two, we took him to see his very first movie in the theater: *Monsters, Inc*. Miles was instantly in love with it. *Monsters, Inc*. became his life; Mike and Sully, the two main characters, were his new BFFs. Over the next few months, our house became littered with every *Monsters, Inc*. piece of paraphernalia ever created.

About a year later, we took Miles to *Finding Nemo*. As a *Monsters, Inc*. loyalist, he had absolutely no interest in a movie about fish. As Miles lay on the floor of the theater lobby in full tantrum mode, refusing to see a movie about anything but monsters, I was this close to losing my shit. I carried him kicking and screaming into the theater. But as it happened, we walked in about a minute into the film, during the scene where Nemo's mom is chomped by a barracuda. This would normally be a scary thing for a three-year old, but not my kid who loved monsters!

Miles was instantly hooked. Much like his first experience with *Monsters, Inc.*, he fell completely in love with *Finding Nemo*.

I could repeat this story for the next several Pixar films. It took until my son was seven or eight to realize he might actually like the next film. He was so stuck in his ways, refusing to accept the possibility of any other option.

The reason I tell this story goes back to the idea that you can't teach an old dog new tricks. As I've already said, people do learn new tricks all the time. And learning them is something we actually resist from a very young age. As my son's story proves, we do not wait until we're old to resist learning something outside our comfort zone. But with enough encouragement and coaching, anyone can learn to adapt to something new, even my stubborn three-year old.

For some people like my good friend who sought my investment advice, it's challenging to break away from obsolete buy-and-hold (and hope!) investment advice. It's easy to stay with what feels familiar. But mixing feelings and emotions with your decisions about your retirement savings is very dangerous business. Nothing can lead to bad financial decisions more than allowing emotion to creep into the process.

Buy-hold-and-hope investing worked during the longest bull market in history, from 1984-1999. But that bull was preceded and followed by decades of stagnant returns, costing investors billions of dollars in lost retirement savings.

I'm coming across more and more people today who are pretty sure that *hope* is not the strategy they want to bet their retirement on. They're motivated to break away from traditional Wall Street thinking. They realize the reality that retirement is on their shoulders and they can't risk blowing it by relying on hope.

Are you sick and tired of riding the market waves up and down hoping it all works out for you one day? Have you ever looked at your portfolio or 401(k) statement and wondered if there was a better way to manage it all?

If you answered "yes" to either question, it's time for you to consider another option.

You can gain control of your retirement savings. You can retire on your terms. And there absolutely is a better way to manage it all. More on that soon, I promise. But first, let's look at a couple more stories as evidence of forward-thinking leadership and learning new ways of doing business.

About six hours northwest of New York City is Rochester, infamously known for its bitter cold winters. Rochester is also known for being the home of two deeply-rooted names in corporate American history: Xerox and Kodak.

Both these companies have struggled greatly as 21st century America has embraced the digital age. Kodak was once synonymous with photography. Despite holding many patents, the company is now for sale to the highest bidder as a result of its failure to modernize and embrace the digital movement. The bottom line for Kodak is that the old dog refused to learn new tricks.

The same could also be said about Xerox, which started digging in its corporate heels during the late 1990s. They were going to remain a document company no matter what--another old dog refusing (at first) to learn new tricks. Although Xerox made some smart acquisitions and the company is now back on track to provide steady growth, it had a shaky transition into the 21st century.

What is the lesson to learn from both Kodak and Xerox? Both were mega-corporations, accounting for tens of thousands of jobs and providing prosperity for much of Greater Rochester. A culture of leadership that refused to adapt as markets and customers' needs changed ultimately cost that great community much of the opulence those companies once created.

Thankfully, not all old corporations think like old dogs that refuse to learn a new trick or two. Recently Google, Intel, and luxury watchmaker TAG Heuer created a partnership to launch an Android-based smartwatch, promising an elegant alternative to the Apple Watch. Jean-Claude Biver, CEO of TAG Heuer, called the partnership "a marriage of technological innovation with watchmaking credibility[37]." What excites me most about this announcement is that TAG Heuer is a Swiss watchmaker that has been at it since 1860! Talk about an old dog learning a new trick. A 155-year old company teams up with some of the most modern and youthful technology organizations to combine classic and elegant with modern and cutting-edge. That's very cool, and it clearly demonstrates forward-thinking leadership.

There is a similar lesson to be learned in the space of planning a secure retirement. Old dogs that refuse to accept that the face of retirement planning has radically changed will wake up one day looking like Kodak, a nearly-defunct organization. Today, pensions have all but disappeared, forcing people to do their own heavy lifting when it comes to looking forward at retirement planning. The big mutual fund companies attempted to "assist" by jumping into the 401(k) business in the 1980s. There were huge profits to be made by fund companies for entering this market, especially if retirement savers automatically added money every month and kept it all fully invested.

The fees charged and earned by the big fund companies became enormous, and their marketing tactics kept the majority of retirement savers sitting still, quietly riding the market waves up and down.

The entrance of the 21st century created the catalyst for change when it came to planning for a secure retirement. The "lost decade" of 2000-2009 proved that 20th century mainstream advice--simple asset allocation, diversification, buy-and-hold investing--didn't work for an aging baby boom population of nearly 81 million investors. In particular, 401(k) savers were left with gaping losses, and many who planned to retire could not.

The good news is that 401(k) savers no longer have to rely on old-dog advice from old-dog Wall Street brokerage firms and mutual fund companies. This is one of the primary reasons why my business partner and I created our firm: to give 401(k) savers the ongoing, personalized advice they deserve to protect their most important retirement assets. Unlike the big Wall Street brokerage firms, we get you. We *are* you.

As I said earlier in this chapter, I've been told countless times over my twenty-year career that you cannot teach old dogs new tricks. I don't buy it, because the only constant in this world is change. Everyone is capable of learning something new, adapting, and being prepared for what comes next. Fortunately for Rochester, Xerox has finally figured that out. A 155-year old watch-maker has also figured it out.

Have you? If you're still riding the market up and down hoping it all works out one day, think again. What happens to your retirement if Wall Street is wrong? What happens to all the plans you've made and the dreams you've dreamt if the next big bear market happens the year before you plan to retire? What would the consequences be for you, your family, your health, your legacy?

ABILITY TO ADAPT TO CHANGE DETERMINES IF AN OLD DOG IS CAPABLE OF LEARNING NEW TRICKS (FINDING NEMO)

OLD DOG

CHANGE → OPEN TO CHANGE →  DOES ADAPT

FINDS NEMO

RESISTS CHANGE

LEFT WATCHING HISTORY REPEAT ITSELF

DOES NOT ADAPT

Peyton Manning of the Denver Broncos is one of the most recognized quarterbacks in the NFL, and quite possibly the best quarterback of all time. He holds fifteen passing records as a quarterback, including the most passing yards in the history of the game.

His brother Eli, of the New York Giants, has not received nearly the same recognition. Yet he has something his brother does not have: two Super Bowl Championships. A top-notch, record-breaking quarterback with a superstar offense can win lots of games, but an average quarterback with the best defense in the NFL can win multiple Super Bowl Championships.

It is an indisputable fact: Offense wins ball games. Defense wins championships.

The same can be said about saving for retirement. Wall Street brokers have promoted buy-and-hold as an all-offense strategy. Buy-and-hold calls for you to stay fully invested at all times, riding the market up and down, hoping it works out one day. You will win some "games," especially during extended bull markets like in the 1990s. But this strategy is also what cost investors major "penalty yards," for example, 20-60% of their retirement savings when the "Bears" came to town in the 1960s, 1970s, 1980's, 2000-2002, and 2008-2009.

Are you ready to challenge Wall Street's call?

The same can be said about my beloved New York Mets and their bid for a 2015 World Series Championship. Mets pitching was really good. Even with a very young pitching staff, they were hard to beat in 2015 and stand to dominate for years ahead (assuming they stay healthy). But 2015 was all about the Mets' bats; their offense was second to none. Outscoring opponents by wide margins in the second half of the season, the bats of the New York Mets propelled them through the National League playoffs and into the World Series.

Yet it was here that my dreams of a world championship crumbled. The Mets defense had completely cracked and cost them dearly. Error after error and repeated poor judgment on defense paved the way for the Kansas City Royals to be crowned world champions in 2015.

Offense wins ballgames. Defense wins championships.

My business partner and I believe that winning the retirement championship requires a strategy that plays both offense and defense, with the ability to transition from one to another on a dime. For millions of 401(k) savers relying on an "all-offense" strategy to win, staying fully invested in a buy-hold-hope approach to 401(k) savings, there are now alternatives. Clients in our private practice seek us out because they want to play defense; we have a common mindset and belief system when it comes to managing risk. The same holds true for 401(k) savers we meet. We all want more than just the status quo of an all-offense strategy for retirement.

Have you ever crept along during freeway rush hour, watching a complete knucklehead rip through traffic like he was the only one on the road? Recently on my commute home from the office, I got a full dose of one of those knuckleheads.

Sammy Speedster came up in my rear-view mirror with those halogen headlamps that catch your attention a mile away. As he blazed past I saw that he was driving one of my absolute favorite cars: a beautiful red Corvette. Boy-oh-boy, was Sammy Speedster flying through traffic. It was if his brand new beauty was built without any brakes.

And then it happened. Right in front of my eyes, skid, swipe, crash! Sammy Speedster clipped a minivan, spun wildly out of control, and blasted head-on into the center divider of the freeway. Traffic that was already tiptoeing along came to a screeching halt.

As much as everyone was cursing this maniac, you could feel the collective sigh of relief that no one was seriously injured. As I drove by the one-car wreck, Sammy Speedster emerged, stomping like a child that had just lost his favorite teddy bear. His beautiful Corvette was totaled. Sammy's public display of hysterics was almost epic.

Hopefully the biggest lesson Sammy learned that day is that there's another pedal on the floor right next to the gas pedal.

It's called *the brake*.

Investors often behave a lot like Sammy Speedster. Drivers receive driver's education and must pass safety exams to own a driver's license. But the law does not require investors to get a license and pass a qualifying exam to drive their retirement savings. Maybe the law should. Instead, investors show up on the first day of work, enroll in this thing called a 401(k), get some advice from a co-worker or a family member about what to drive (invest in), and then Wall Street brokerage firms "educate" them on how to drive.

Most 401(k) investors are taught from day one to put their foot on the gas pedal and keep it there until they retire. It's the message Wall Street brokerage firms have shared for decades. It's a strategy we've discussed throughout the book, called "buy and hold," or as we like to call it, "buy-hold-and-hope." Wall Street brokers preach that it's a long road trip and you have to get comfortable dealing with road hazards and accidents along the way; that if you think long-term, hoping you get there safely, it should all work out one day.

This approach worked incredibly well during the twenty-year stretch of open highway in the 1980s and 1990s. It was the greatest bull market in history. But since then, the "All Gas, No Brake" method of driving one's retirement has created disastrous consequences for millions of retirement savers, many of whom were very close to their final destination.

There's a reason your car has brakes, and contrary to popular Wall Street thinking, your 401(k) has brakes too. You just may not be aware of how to use them.

Markets have been recently flirting with all-time highs. The devastating multi-vehicle crash of 2008 is too far in the rear-view mirror to remember what caused it, and too many investors have been driving their 401(k) with their foot on the gas ever since.

I'm not suggesting another 2008 market is imminent. Markets could continue to move higher for weeks, months, or even years. Historically, markets reach highs and eventually experience some sort of pullback, whether it's a fender bender-like correction of 10-15%, or a full-blown multi-car freeway wreck like we had in 2000, 2001, 2002, and 2008 (boy, that's a lot of big wrecks in the past fifteen years!).

Are you willing to wait until an accident happens again before you adjust your driving strategy? Should you consider learning how to tap the brakes of your 401(k), so when the positive trends reverse, you're prepared?

After building a private wealth management practice, my business partner and I turned to building a second business, meant to serve many more people. We are building a mechanism you could call an "online GPS tool." It's built to give you customized, turn-by-turn instructions on what to own inside your 401(k) plan each and every quarter. It will even tell you when it's time to have your foot on the gas pedal or when it's time to tap the brakes and move to cash. Outside of a few quarterly adjustments that will take no time for you to implement, your primary job is to sit back and enjoy the drive.

My business partner and I have been managing our private clients' assets this way for many years. But there are only so many families we can work with individually. The retirement highway is a dangerous game. We felt it was our responsibility to build a cost-effective way to offer this type of "driving" to millions of retirement savers.

Whether you are just getting started with your 401(k), or you're a seasoned investor with a lot to lose if you crash your car, it's time to focus on defensive driving for your most significant retirement asset.

I wrote this book because millions of people are suffering quietly as I did. Life looks great on the outside, but the pain inside is unbearable. This pain affects all aspects of life, especially within close personal relationships, satisfaction and success at work, the ability to have real fun in life, and often creates a very misguided belief system about money. The effects can ruin the family budget, or even destroy the hopes of growing a sizable 401(k) savings account.

If this book helps a few people take off their masks and live a more authentic, abundant, wealthy life, than I will have done my job.

My purpose in life, my reason for existence, is to challenge the status quo and show others how to do the same. I have developed a unique belief system about money, true wealth and living authentically. It wasn't easy to allow myself to be completely vulnerable to everyone. But maybe, like me, you have spent years or possibly decades lying to yourself and others. The lies and deception run so deep that you may even believe them to be your real-life story. If this is you, I feel your hurt. I feel your shame. Maybe it's led you to a life of substance abuse or compulsive spending like it did me. But besides the anguish, I also feel the glow of a beautiful person hiding behind that mask, someone who wants to give their gifts to the world; a person who is starving for acceptance and a simpler life of true wealth and genuine happiness. By taking off your mask, you've taken a huge first step. You should be very proud of yourself. It's scary, I know.

You might wonder "what if the world finds out I'm just a pathetic loser without two nickels to rub together? Or that I'm not as smart, or strong, or successful as they all think I am? Will I be shunned? Will I be all alone?"

All I can say is that as you peel back the layers the real you has been hiding behind and finally remove your mask, some doors will close and others will open. Finding the path to true wealth and happiness will invite those who are meant to be in your life and repel those who are not.

Be brave. Have faith. Everything you need to be complete is already within you.

It's time to take it off.

ABOUT THE AUTHOR

Matthew D. Grishman

AUTHOR, SPEAKER AND WEALTH COACH. CO-FOUNDER OF 401(K) MASTERS, LLC. PRINCIPAL/WEALTH ADVISOR OF GEBHARDT GROUP, INC.

Coaching is Matthew's passion. He is obsessed with challenging the status quo and teaching others how to do the same. Matthew has developed a unique belief system about money and true wealth that runs completely counter to the Wall Street culture in which he was raised. His unique ability is to inspire people to live abundantly and authentically. Whether Matthew is helping a family define and protect their true wealth, guiding other wealth advisors to discover their own value proposition, or teaching the youth in his community about life through the games of baseball and basketball, Matthew shows up and gives it his all each and every day.

Matthew began his career in financial services in 1995 with A.G. Edwards & Sons, Inc., and became fully licensed as an Investment Broker in 1996. He spent seventeen years as a national spokesperson for large mutual fund and insurance companies (Lord, Abbett & Co, Putnam, and MetLife).

Matthew left corporate America in 2011 to devote his time and experience in financial services to his family, friends and neighbors. In 2014, Matthew joined Gebhardt Group, Inc., an independent Registered Investment Advisor. He became an owner of the firm in 2015. As a Principal and Wealth Advisor of Gebhardt Group, Inc., Matthew provides wealth management services for families experiencing major life transitions (e.g. inheritance, sale of a business, death or divorce of a spouse, planning for retirement, career change, or sudden loss of employment).

Matthew is also the Co-Founder and Chief Marketing Officer of the 401(k) advisory service 401(k) Masters, LLC. He leads the company's Sacramento-area office.

Matthew resides with his wife, Amie, and their two sons, Miles and Lucas, in Rocklin, California. When not working with clients, Matthew spends his time exploring amazing places with his family, like Yosemite National Park, the California Coast, and big cities around the world. Matthew is a volunteer umpire and baseball coach for his local Little League. He also served for eight years on their Board of Directors.

Matthew received a Bachelor of Arts degree in Political Science and Sociology from the State University of New York at Albany in Albany, New York in June of 1994. He holds a State of California Insurance License for Life, Accident, Disability and Health Insurance. His registrations include the Series 65.

WORKS CITED

[1] https://www.fidelity.com/static/dcle/welcome/documents/CouplesRetirementStudy.pdf

[2] http://pages.stern.nyu.edu/~adamodar/New_Home_Page/datafile/histretSP.html

[3] http://www.bankrate.com/finance/cd/rate-roundup.aspx

[4] http://inflationdata.com/Inflation/Inflation_Rate/Long_Term_Inflation.asp

[5] http://observationsandnotes.blogspot.com/2010/11/100-years-of-bond-interest-rate-history.html

[6] http://treasurydirect.gov/

[7] http://www.cfp.net/

[8] http://www.wiseradvisor.com/

[9] http://brokercheck.finra.org/

[10] http://www.icifactbook.org/fb_data.html

[11, 12, 13] http://www.forbes.com/2011/04/04/real-cost-mutual-fund-taxes-fees-retirement-bernicke.html

[14] http://www.wsj.com/articles/SB10001424053111904583204576544681577401622

[15] http://www.cbsnews.com/news/social-securitys-new-report-has-a-clear-message/

[16] http://demog.berkeley.edu/~andrew/1918/%20figure2.html

[17] https://www.ssa.gov/history/ratios.html

[18] http://en.wikipedia.org/wiki/Retirement

[19] http://www.merriam-webster.com/dictionary/retirement

[20] http://www.401(k)masters.com/landing-page.html

[21] http://www.forbes.com/sites/nextavenue/2013/06/10/how-much-to-withdraw-from-retirement-savings/

[22] http://www.cnbc.com/id/100822251

[23] http://www.cnbc.com/2015/05/22/medical-cost-inflation-highest-level-in-8-years.html

[24] http://www.city-data.com/forum/california/1497767-california-divorce-rate-75-a.html

[25] http://www.geoba.se/country.php?cc=US&year=2014

[26] http://www.wiserwomen.org/

[27] http://www.finra.org/brokercheck

[28] http://www.nytimes.com/2015/05/17/upshot/dont-be-so-sure-the-economy-will-return-to-normal.html?_r=0

[29] http://www.401(k)masters.com/enroll-now.html

[30] http://www.401(k)masters.com/blog-page/2015/04/22/fool-me-once-shame-on-you-fool-me-twice/

[31] http://www.advisorperspectives.com/dshort/updates/Conference-Board-Consumer-Confidence-Index.php

[32] http://www.reuters.com/article/2015/05/13/us-usa-economy-idUSKBN0NY1HC20150513

[33] http://www.bloomberg.com/news/articles/2015-03-30/u-s-consumers-are-saving-at-highest-rate-since-2012

[34] https://www.fidelity.com/viewpoints/retirement/cashing-out

[35] https://www.ssa.gov/policy/docs/quickfacts/stat_snapshot/

[36] https://en.wikipedia.org/wiki/2002_Oakland_Athletics_season

[37] http://www.usatoday.com/story/tech/columnist/baig/2015/03/19/google-teams-with-intel-tag-heuer-on-android-wear-watches/25005043/

www.ingramcontent.com/pod-product-compliance
Lightning Source LLC
Chambersburg PA
CBHW022037190326
41520CB00008B/611